The Existence and Nature of God

UNIVERSITY OF NOTRE DAME
STUDIES IN THE
PHILOSOPHY OF RELIGION

Number 3

The Existence and Nature of God

Edited with an Introduction by
ALFRED J. FREDDOSO

UNIVERSITY OF NOTRE DAME PRESS

NOTRE DAME   LONDON

Library of Congress Cataloging in Publication Data

Main entry under title:

The Existence and nature of God.

(University of Notre Dame studies in the
philosophy of religion ; v. 3)
    Includes bibliographical references.
    1. God—Addresses, essays, lectures.
I. Freddoso, Alfred J.   II. Series.
BT102.E92   1983   212   83-47521
ISBN 0-268-00910-4

Manufactured in the United States of America

Contents

Contributors

CLEMENT DORE is Professor of Philosophy at Vanderbilt University. He is the author of many journal articles on topics in the philosophy of religion, especially on the problem of evil.

THOMAS P. FLINT is Harper Instructor in the Humanities at the University of Chicago. His publications include papers in epistemology and philosophy of religion.

ALFRED J. FREDDOSO is Assistant Professor of Philosophy at the University of Notre Dame. He cotranslated and introduced *Ockham's Theory of Propositions* and has published papers in metaphysics and medieval philosophy.

MARK D. JORDAN is Assistant Professor of Philosophy at the University of Dallas. His publications include several papers on Aquinas's metaphysics and modes of discourse.

NELSON PIKE is Professor of Philosophy at the University of California, Irvine. He is the author of *God and Timelessness* and the editor of *God and Evil* and of Hume's *Dialogues Concerning Natural Religion*. In addition he has published numerous papers in the philosophy of religion.

PHILIP L. QUINN is Professor of Philosophy at Brown University. He is the author of *Divine Commands and Moral Requirements* and of many journal articles in the philosophy of religion, philosophy of science, and metaphysics.

JAMES F. ROSS is Professor of Philosophy at the University of Pennsylvania. He has written several books in the philosophy of religion, including *Introduction to Philosophy of*

Religion, *Philosophical Theology*, and *Portraying Analogy*. He also edited *Inquiries into Medieval Philosophy* and translated and introduced Suarez's *On Formal and Universal Unity*. In addition he is the author of many journal articles.

RICHARD SWINBURNE is Professor of Philosophy at the University of Keele. He is the author of *The Concept of Miracle* as well as of the recently completed trilogy consisting of *The Coherence of Theism*, *The Existence of God*, and *Faith and Reason*. In addition to his copious work in the philosophy of religion, he has also published several books on topics in the philosophy of science.

Introduction

ALFRED J. FREDDOSO

Some contemporary theologians dismiss the classical discussions of the existence and nature of God as out of step with and unworthy of serious consideration by so-called "modern man." Others contend that even though the historical giants of philosophical theology generally had an intimate acquaintance with Sacred Scripture, their philosophical biases beguiled them unwittingly into forming conceptions of God that are wholly foreign to as well as incompatible with the biblical conception of God. These two distinct lines of criticism sometimes converge in the suggestion that today's philosophical theologians should forsake their old heroes for duly modern ones like Whitehead, Heidegger, and Wittgenstein, whose writings allegedly provide philosophical outlooks more in tune with biblical categories of thought. Just as often, however, we find an attitude of distrust toward any sort of metaphysical reflection on the ostensible theological claims of the Judaeo-Christian tradition—both on the part of those who believe that the Judaeo-Christian myths have at most only ethical and perhaps political significance and on the part of those who believe that metaphysical inquiry invariably distorts theological truths by displacing Sacred Scripture as the foundation of the life of faith. Despite their disagreements, however, all sides concur in assigning little if any systematic importance to traditional philosophical theology.

In light of this it is at least mildly surprising that a growing number of Anglo-American philosophers, many of them highly distinguished, are finding the classical discussions of God's existence and nature to be fertile sources for critical reflection on issues in the philosophy of religion. Perhaps these philosophers merely constitute the residue of an outmoded and long-since transcended intellectual era. Perhaps they lack a proper sensitivity to biblical theology. Perhaps, on the other hand, they have discovered something of authentic and enduring significance for the life of faith in the works of their philosophical and theological ancestors. Whatever the correct assessment might be, the papers which follow are representative of this contemporary, if not "modern," interest in the classical arguments for God's existence and in the attributes traditionally ascribed to God. Though the topics vary, the authors without exception see themselves as working within the tradition established by St. Augustine, Pseudo-Dionysius, St. Anselm, Moses Maimonides, St. Thomas Aquinas, John Duns Scotus, William of Ockham, John Calvin, Luis de Molina, Descartes, Leibniz, Jonathan Edwards, and other eminent historical figures cited in both text and footnotes.

The first two papers deal with the problem of evil, broadly speaking. In "Over-Power and God's Responsibility for Sin" Nelson Pike focuses on the traditional Christian belief that God has complete control over what occurs in the realm of creation. He begins by arguing against recent critics that this belief about God's power is compatible with the claim that human beings are free and hence have power of their own. Using a series of wiring diagrams as models, Pike develops the concept of "over-power." God's over-power consists in his having the power to endow creatures with their own power and to allow them to control certain events. But even though God can thus refrain from exercising his own control over some events, his over-power, Pike contends, renders him responsible for sin. This becomes clear when we reflect on mundane examples of over-power which involve dual-control automobiles of the sort used in driver-education classes. When accidents occur, the instructor clearly shares responsibility for them, since he has the power to prevent them. In the same way God shares responsibility for the sins of his creatures. For their power, though genuine, is conditional. God could prevent them from sinning if he so willed.

This fact has immediate consequences for the apologetic task of devising responses to the problem of evil. Since, as Pike sees it, the central claim of free-will theodicies like those suggested by Aquinas and, more recently, Alvin Plantinga is that God is not responsible for sin, such theodicies must fail. In short, their proponents fail to take into account the full scope of the divine power. Of course, it is a further question whether God is *blameworthy* as well as responsible for allowing created agents to act immorally. On this point Pike argues that a classical Augustinian theodicy, according to which immoral actions (like other evils) are morally tolerable because of their contribution to some ultimate good, offers the most promising line of defense for the Christian apologist who correctly understands the extent of God's power.

Evelyn Waugh once wrote that the most common question asked him by agnostics was "Do you believe in hell?" This is not surprising, despite the fact that the doctrine of hell has generally received rather superficial treatment in recent theology. For there is ample reason for thinking that ultimately the most troublesome form which the problem of evil can take for the orthodox Christian is just this: How is the existence of a benevolent and almighty God to be reconciled with even the possibility of someone's going to hell (whether this is thought to involve simple annihilation or the pain of everlasting separation from God)? Richard Swinburne addresses just this question in "A Theodicy of Heaven and Hell."

Swinburne commences by defending the traditional claim that both correct belief and good will ("faith formed by love") are required for entry into heaven. For, he argues, careful reflection on our ordinary conception of happiness reveals that both of these elements are needed for supreme happiness — and Christianity identifies the vision of God in heaven with the supreme happiness of human beings. Now God can properly grant, after their deaths, true belief to those persons of good will who through no fault of their own have failed to acquire the correct religious beliefs in this life. But the case of someone with bad will is altogether different. Given the reality of original sin and the nature of human choice, it appears quite possible that some human being might continually reject God's grace and in the end find himself utterly incapable of controlling or resisting his sinful desires. Such a totally corrupt person would neither desire the vision of God nor be able to enjoy it. And, Swinburne continues, it would be wrong for God to change such a person's desires against his will, and also wrong for God to prevent human beings from becoming utterly depraved and hence hellbound in the first place. Nor, he argues at some length, would it necessarily help a person gain salvation if God made it absolutely clear to him that heaven exists and is accessible only to someone with a good character. Hence, it is reasonable to conclude that the everlasting separation of the virtuous from the wicked is indeed compatible with God's goodness.

The next three papers have as their central concern the nature and extent of God's power. In "Divine Conservation, Continuous Creation, and Human Action" Philip Quinn proposes to find out whether there is a plausible construal of the notions of creation and conservation that will sustain the thesis, asserted by many classical theistic philosophers, that God's conserving things in existence is no different from his continuously creating them. Intuitively God creates a thing just in case he causes it to exist at a time before which it has not existed, and God's conserving a thing is equivalent to that thing's having existence at any given time if and only if God causes it to exist at that time. Unfortunately, these definitions lead to rather implausible conclusions when we go on to make the traditional conjunctive claim that God conserves each contingent thing and that conservation is equivalent to continuous creation. For it follows directly that no creature which begins to exist exists for more than a single moment. Though Jonathan Edwards welcomed this consequence in his inventive attempt to explicate the doctrine of original sin, Quinn argues that it entails the absurd thesis that no human action (including, ironically, the sin of Adam) is so much as possible.

After briefly examining some remarks of Duns Scotus on the ordinary meanings of the terms 'create' and 'conserve', Quinn departs from linguistic orthodoxy by suggesting a second theory, according to which creation and conservation are taken to be definitionally equivalent. God creates (conserves) a thing at a given time just in case he causes it to exist at that time—regardless of whether it has previously existed. Though intuitively less satisfying than its predecessor, this theory captures perfectly the idea that conservation involves just the same sort of power and activity on God's part that creation does. And it also has the desired consequence that God's continuously creating a persistent thing is both possible and also equivalent to his conserving it in existence through a continuous interval of time. Furthermore, the ordinary notions of creation and conservation explicated by Scotus can readily be defined in terms of the technical analogues of those notions which ground this second theory. The net result, Quinn claims, is a theory about conservation and continuous creation that is both defensible and deserving of further attention by philosophers of religion.

The formulation of an adequate analysis of omnipotence has been the object of a great deal of recent work in philosophical theology. However, no one has succeeded in fashioning an analysis which is both philosophically adequate and consistent with the traditional theological assertion that God is omnipotent and yet also incapable of acting in a morally reprehensible way. In fact, Peter Geach has gone so far as to surmise that any philosophically acceptable account of omnipotence will imply that in order to be omnipotent a being must be able to act immorally. This does not trouble Geach, since he denies that belief in God's omnipotence (as opposed to his almightiness) is an element of Christian orthodoxy. By contrast, Nelson Pike draws the opposite — and less obviously orthodox — conclusion that because the person who is God is omnipotent, he does not lack the power to sin. In "Maximal Power" Thomas Flint and I propose to show that this alleged theological problem of the conflict between omnipotence and impeccability evaporates precisely when a philosophically adequate account of omnipotence arrives on the scene.

We begin by putting forward and discussing in some detail five conditions of philosophical adequacy for an analysis of omnipotence, paying special attention to (a) the distinction between a weak and a strong sense in which agents actualize states of affairs, (b) the purely temporal constraints on any agent's power, and (c) the constraints on any agent's power which are imposed by truths about how other agents would freely act in various hypothetical circumstances. The analysis then presented satisfies, we claim, each of these conditions and in addition escapes the dreaded paradoxes of omnipotence. We then argue in some detail that given our analysis of omnipotence, there is no problem with the claim that God is both essentially omnipotent and essentially impeccable. There are some evil states of affairs that God can actualize (in at least the weak sense) without being morally blameworthy. There are others which he cannot actualize — but this does not undermine his omnipotence, since such states of affairs cannot be actualized by anyone if an essentially divine being exists. Finally, we show that our analysis does not require that in order to be omnipotent God must have the power to break his previously made promises.

James Ross's intriguing "Creation II" appropriately follows the paper just discussed, since Ross's main purpose is to dislodge the assumption that God's power is properly and adequately thought of as the power to cause (or bring about or actualize) states of affairs. This mistaken picture of the nature of God's power, he claims, leads easily to an assimilation of God's causation to ordinary physical causation and thus generates artificial paradoxes concerning creation, human freedom, foreknowledge, and God's responsibility for sin. Ross, on the other hand, insists with Aquinas that God's power is, properly speaking, the power to cause being and that God's causation is metaphysical causation, the causation of being. Of course, the power to cause being entails the power to cause states of affairs, but the notion of causation is not univocal over both. The latter sort of power, Ross maintains, is parasitic on the former and causal only in a derivative and rather anemic sense. As a result, one who takes states of affairs to be the primary and proper objects of divine power focuses merely on the shadow-like concomitants of God's causal activity.

Although God's power is distinctive, Ross contends here, as in earlier works, that there are more familiar instances of metaphysical causation which can serve as instructive (if imperfect) analogues of God's causal activity. Here he pays particular attention to the causality exercised by the abstract mathematical structures of physical objects on the behavior of such objects. This example is especially interesting, since these abstract structures provide the metaphysical foundation for ordinary nomological regularities and laws. So even in the realm of nature metaphysical causation is basic. In the theological case God creates and sustains substances which are "from-him" and hence always and everywhere dependent on him for their being — even though they possess their own proper existence and power.

In the last part of his paper Ross tries to demonstrate how this picture of God's causation obviates some of the problems which are needlessly generated by the "states-of-affairs" picture. For instance, on the latter picture we can say only that God causes it to be the case that Adam freely sins. And hence the inevitable questions arise: Can Adam do otherwise? Is God the author of Adam's sin? Perhaps the proponent of the "states-of-affairs" picture will respond by distinguishing weaker and stronger modes of God's causal activity. But Ross retorts that God's causal activity is essentially uniform — only the objects of that activity, viz., the things created, may vary. On the metaphysical causation picture God causes Adam, who freely sins, to be. Adam could refrain from sinning, in which case God would cause Adam to be in exactly the same say in which he in fact causes Adam to be. Adam's action alone would be different. Further, Adam's sinful action is Adam's action and not God's, even though God causes Adam to be during the performance of that action. Hence, God is not responsible for or the author of Adam's sin. In the same way, Ross holds, various puzzles about God's reasons for creating and his choice of a world to create fall to the wayside on the metaphysical causation picture.

There is undoubtedly more to be said on these issues, but Ross's position has a weighty tradition behind it and is deserving of serious consideration. Interestingly, one can detect in the contrast between "Creation II" and "Maximal Power" at least a hint of the same disagreements about divine causation that separated Thomists from Molinists in sixteenth-century Catholic theology.

The next paper, Clement Dore's "Descartes's Meditation V Proof of God's Existence," is an attempt to reinterpret and defend an argument which has been almost universally found wanting since the time of Descartes. Dore begins by conceding the defectiveness of the following classical construal of the argument:

    (1) God is a supremely perfect being.
    (2) Existence is a perfection (relative to God).
So   (3) God really exists.

Though Kant's famous objection to this argument was aimed at (2), Dore assumes throughout that (2) is true. (This is not unreasonable, since many today find Kant's attempted refutation of (2) rather unconvincing.) The genuinely troublesome premise is (1), since on the most natural reading (1) is equivalent to

(1*) If God exists, then he is a supremely perfect being,

which together with (2) entails only the "ontologically sterile" conditional

(3*) If God exists, then he exists.

Dore, however, urges that we adopt the following, "more charitable" interpretation of Descartes's argument:

- (4) The concept of God is the concept of a supremely perfect being.
- (5) The concept of existence is the concept of a perfection (relative to God).
- So (6) It is a conceptual truth that God exists.
- So (7) God really exists.

The remainder of the paper is devoted to the refutation of a series of seemingly powerful objections to this argument, two of which I will mention briefly. According to the first objection the argument is invalid because (6) expresses just what the ontologically sterile (3*) expresses. Dore's central counterargument here is that conceptual truths, unlike mere logical truths, depend essentially for their truth on the peculiar properties of their material, nonlogical terms. Hence, (6) is true only if some syntactically appropriate substitution for the term 'God' in the sentence 'God exists' yields a falsehood. On the other hand, any syntactically appropriate substitution for the term 'God' in (3*) yields a truth. It follows that (6) does not express exactly what the logical truth (3*) expresses. The second objection is a Gaunilo-inspired direct attack on (6). It charges that if (6) were true, then we could deduce the existence of indefinitely many Godlike minor and major deities by using exactly the same argument form exhibited by (4)-(7). Dore counters that if God exists, then the existence of such ersatz deities is logically impossible, and so the analogues of (6) in the resulting equiform arguments are without exception false. But, he contends, there is no analogously effective way of showing that (6) itself is false.

The remaining objections are greeted with similarly interesting retorts. In short, whether or not he has been completely successful in his venture, Dore has without a doubt breathed some life into what has generally been thought to be a dead argument.

Mark Jordan's "The Names of God and the Being of Names" is an apt concluding piece, since it calls into question what some might construe as facile presuppositions in some of the previous papers about the accessibility of the divine nature to human language and understanding. Medieval theologians typically preface their discussions of the divine attributes with warnings about the inability of the divine names to "make the signified present." Jordan's purpose is to argue, with Aquinas as his main protagonist, that the most secure theological approach to the divine lies precisely in the attempt to understand how the divine names, while truly signifying God, can at the same time mark the distance which separates us from God.

Aquinas's scattered remarks about analogy are often thought to exhaust his account of theological language. Jordan, however, insists that Aquinas turns to semantics only after he has established the metaphysical thesis that God is simple, lacking (passive) potency and hence composition of any sort. It is because of God's simplicity that even the patently nonmetaphorical ascriptions made of him will fail to signify him in the normal mode. For Aquinas believes that since all the names ascribed to God are taken from creatures, they connote composition on the part of their subjects. Hence, God's simplicity rules out from the beginning any form of literalism.

On the other hand, the notion of simplicity generates a hierarchical ordering of the divine names, since some of those names are more appropriately applied to a simple being than are others. Jordan points out that this hierarchy of names also has a metaphysical foundation. For Aquinas believes that creatures, as effects, bear greater and lesser resemblances to God as their cause. When theologians deemphasize or ignore such essential resemblances, they quickly fall into obscurantist views — like that attributed by Aquinas to Maimonides — according to which every apparently affirmative ascription of a divine perfection to God is in reality just the denial of some creaturely imperfection. This position, Aquinas argues, leads to theological anarchy by rendering all the divine names equally improper.

Aquinas finds in the writings of Pseudo-Dionysius the framework for an acceptable *via media* that preserves both of the metaphysical theses noted above. In virtue of the varying degrees of resemblance between God and creatures, we may properly (and not just metaphorically) affirm certain "higher" names of God, as when we say that God is wise. Such affirmations, Jordan notes, are not simply disguised negations. Negation comes only at the next step, when — because of God's simplicity — we deny that God is wise. For, as noted above, the term 'wise' in its normal mode of signifcation connotes composition and hence imperfection on the part of its subject. Finally, we signal God's distance from us more positively by the grammatically deviant assertion that God is unparticipated wisdom itself. So it is precisely within this progression through the ways of affirmation, negation, and eminence that we gain insight into how the divine names succeed in signifying God (for creatures are imitations of his essence) and yet fail to signify him in a normal way (for he is simple).

In contemporary philosophical theology one finds widespread evidence of the two extremes, literalism and obscurantism, which Aquinas sought to avoid. Further, the doctrine of divine simplicity and the thesis that effects resemble their causes have been generally ignored or, at best, afforded superficial treatment. If Jordan is correct, these two phenomena are not unconnected.

The papers in this volume, then, reflect the lively, yet tradition-laden, character of at least one major current in contemporary philosophical theology. At a time when many theologians have in effect discarded as irrelevant large chunks of traditional philosophical theology, it may be the unlikely lot of contemporary philosophers to crack open once again the lonely dust-covered volumes.

One final note. Earlier versions of these papers were presented at the third biennial Notre Dame Conference on Philosophy of Religion in April 1981. Commentators included William Alston, Richard Ciccotelli, Ralph McInerny, Alvin Plantinga, William Rowe, Patrick Sherry, and William Wainwright. Their contributions both to the conference and to the final state of this volume have been enormous.

Over-Power and God's Responsibility for Sin

NELSON PIKE

I shall assume that if God exists and is omnipotent, then with respect to any possible event (E) God has power sufficient to determine whether or not E occurs. This is to say that if God exists and is omnipotent, he has control with respect to the occurrence or nonoccurrence of every possible event. And because it would be hard to find a theologian of consequence in the Western tradition who would not accept this thesis, I shall refer to it throughout as the "traditional" doctrine of divine omnipotence. Now allow that the performance of an action on the part of a created agent counts as an event. It follows that if God exists and is omnipotent, he has power sufficient to determine whether or not a given action is performed by a given agent. God has control even with respect to the actions performed by other beings. What, then, of the power of created agents? In an article published in 1978 entitled "Freedom within Omnipotence," Linwood Urban and Douglas Walton maintain that if omnipotence is understood in the way just suggested, then if there exists an omnipotent being, that being "exhausts all the power in the universe leaving no room for other centers of power." The idea of human freedom to control (even partially) some of the events of the world is, then, what they call an "illusion." The consequence is that created beings cannot be held responsible for anything that happens—not even their own actions. And applying this conclusion to the topic of the problem of evil, Urban and Walton claim: "One can easily see that this result is disastrous for those who hope to solve the problem of

11

evil at least partially by placing the blame for some of the evil in the world upon men."[1] If God alone has power, then he alone is responsible. Given that someone in the world is to be blamed, he is really the only one it could be.

As a general remark, the claim that there is a logical conflict between the idea of creaturely freedom and traditional thinking about the nature of God has usually been argued, not by reference to the doctrine of divine omnipotence, but by reference to the notion of divine omniscience. I here have in mind the problem of divine foreknowledge — an issue widely discussed in antiquity and currently commanding considerable attention among contemporary philosophers. According to Anthony Flew, however, while it is (as he says) "rash" to suggest that divine omniscience (foreknowledge) presents any threat to the idea of human freedom, (in his words) "the problem really begins with omnipotence." Flew continues: "As Creator (God) must be first cause, prime mover, supporter and controller of every thought and action throughout his utterly dependent universe. In short: if creation is in, autonomy is out." This, Flew tells us is a "vital conclusion" that is often ignored.[2] Subsequent discussion makes clear that by "autonomy" Flew means creaturely free will[3] and that it, rather than God considered as omnipotent creator, is definitely in. Precisely this same thesis has been urged by advocates of (so-called) "Process Theology." In the first full-length study of the problem of evil from the (so-called) "process" point of view, David Griffin (following Hartshorne) claims that if God is omnipotent in the traditional sense, then God has "all the power," and this, he says, is quite incompatible with a manifest metaphysical truth, viz., that there are beings other than God with power to determine (partially) their own activities and the activities of other beings.[4] Thus, while the view we are here considering has not enjoyed much in the way of historical visibility, it is among the challenges currently confronting traditional Christian theism. And, of course, if God's omnipotence really is incompatible with creaturely freedom, then Urban and Walton are right in extending the conclusion to a negative judgment on one of the more important theological responses to the problem of evil, i.e., the view that creatures, rather than God, are responsible for at least the portion of the evil in the world that consists in and results from their own, freely chosen, immoral actions.

Though it would have other unfortunate consequences for Christian theology as well, given the abundance of recent literature on the topic of free will and evil, this one would be of very special interest to contemporary philosophers of religion.

In this paper I am going to argue two nested points. First, the doctrine of omnipotence formulated above carries no negative implications as regards the existence of creaturely freedom. Urban and Walton as well as the other philosophers and theologians who have argued to the contrary are wrong about this. But, second, if God is omnipotent in the sense specified above, then any theodicy in which it is held that God is not responsible for the performance of immoral actions on the part of created agents is false. I should add that I regard the second of these points as the central thesis of this paper. The first is argued partly to dispel the misunderstandings of those who have denied it but mostly because the resulting clarification of the notion of divine omnipotence establishes a context in which the second point can be made clear.

Postscript: Throughout I assume that an omnipotent being is one who has power sufficient to determine the occurrence or nonoccurrence of any possible event. I specify the notion of omnipotence in this way rather than in terms of God's ability to bring about possible states of affairs because in this essay I am interested in omnipotence as it relates to *actions*, and I take actions to be events (occurrences, happenings) rather than states of affairs. Further, I realize that the formula I am using to express the notion of omnipotence is subject to a variety of counterexamples. For instance, there are some things that might be thought of as possible events that no being (however powerful) could determine because they are not determinable, e.g., two plus two equalling four. Then, too, the undetermined-event E and the undetermined-by-an-omnipotent-being-event E could not be determined by an omnipotent being. Of particular interest in the present discussion are events involving the free agency of finite beings, e.g., Jones freely raising his arm or Jones freely choosing to raise his arms. I assume that any such event could be determined only by the relevant finite being and thus, like the above, could not be determined by an omnipotent God. I suspect that most counterexamples of this sort could be accommodated were I to specify God's omnipotence as "power sufficient to determine any possible event E where 'God determines E' is consistent." But since the argument of this paper neither depends upon nor (so far as I can see) trespasses against refinements that would be needed to transform the formula I am using into a fully adequate analysis, I shall not invite distraction by trying to work them out and then fumbling to carry them along in the present discussion.

I
Over-Power

I shall begin by developing the concept that will play the leading role in my discussion — the concept of over-power. Here I shall proceed via a series of reflections on four diagrams representing four electrical circuits. This first section might best be thought of as an exercise in a priori electrical engineering — a study of the concept of control in plain and humble physical dress. I hasten to add that this procedure is taken directly from Urban and Walton. The following pieces of technical apparatus are at least inspired by them as well.

Let us agree that an agent has *positive control* with respect to a given event (E) if that agent has power so to act as to make a causal contribution to the occurrence of E. Correlatively, an agent has *negative control* with respect to E if that agent has power so to act as to make a causal contribution to the nonoccurrence of E, i.e., the occurrence of not-E. There are two subcases under each of these. An agent has *full* positive control with respect to E if that agent has power *sufficient* to effect or secure E. An agent has *partial* positive control with respect to E if that agent has power so to act as to supply a *necessary* (though not a sufficient) condition for the occurrence of E. So also for negative control. An agent's negative control is full if that agent has power sufficient to secure not-E. It is partial if it is within that agent's power so to act as to supply a necessary (though not a sufficient) condition for not-E. As a final piece of operating equipment, let us say that an agent has *complete control* with respect to E if that agent has full positive control and full negative control with respect to E.

Now, as a warm-up, consider the two electrical circuits represented by Fig. 1 and Fig. 2. Understand that there are two agents (Arthur and Bailey) stationed at the switches A and B respectively. Allow that Arthur and Bailey are independent agents, i.e., neither can affect the actions of the other. Let E be the bulb pictured at the top of the diagram coming on. Not-E is the bulb going off.

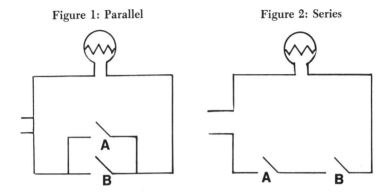

Figure 1: Parallel   Figure 2: Series

In the situation diagramed in Fig. 1 (the parallel circuit) both Arthur and Bailey have full positive control with respect to E. This is because Arthur can effect E by closing A and Bailey can effect E by closing B. However, neither has full negative control. Not-E results only if both switches are open. Thus, in this circumstance both Arthur's and Bailey's negative control is only partial. Thus, neither has complete control with respect to E. In the situation portrayed in Fig. 2 (the series circuit) we get the same final result but in reverse manner. Here Arthur and Bailey both have full negative control but neither has full positive control. This is because each can secure not-E by opening his own switch, but neither can effect E by himself. To effect E both Arthur and Bailey must close their respective switches. Thus, in this case Arthur's positive control and Bailey's positive control are both partial. Hence, again, neither Arthur nor Bailey have complete control with respect to E.

Could we construct a circuit having switches operated by two independent agents and with respect to which one of those agents has complete control as regards E? By itself this would not be difficult, as can be seen in Fig. 3. Here Arthur has complete control. He can effect E by closing A, and he can secure not-E by opening A. And how about Bailey? He can work his switch, but he is not in position to make a causal contribution to the occurrence or nonoccurrence of E. He has been bypassed and thus has no control — full or partial. It is as if we had a circuit with only one switch (A) and Arthur alone to determine whether the light goes on or off.

Figure 3: Bypass

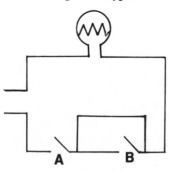

This, then, provokes the next question — one that may be more difficult to answer than the last — viz., could we construct a circuit in which one agent has complete control and in which a second agent has at least some (partial) control with respect to E? This question is of special interest in the present discussion since we are assuming that with respect to any possible event an omnipotent being would have power sufficient to determine the occurrence or nonoccurrence of that event (i.e., complete control). What we would like to know is whether it would make sense to suppose that some other agent could also have some control with respect to some selection of worldly events. It is to this problem that I now turn attention.

Look closely at Fig. 4. Here the circuit represented has three switches instead of two. Switch A_1 is located on the wire pictured in the middle of the diagram, and switches A_2 and B are mounted on the wire portrayed at the bottom. The circuit as a whole might best be thought of as a complex consisting of the situations portrayed in Fig. 1 and Fig. 2 taken together. There is a parallel subcircuit consisting of the wires represented by the middle and bottom lines, and there is also a series circuit set up on the bottom line alone. Now suppose that there are only two agents — Bailey who is in position to work switch B and Arthur who is stationed between A_1 and A_2 and can thus operate both of them at once. We can see right away that Arthur has complete control with respect to E. He has full positive control because if he closes A_1 (A_2 either open or closed), the light goes on. He also has full negative control because if he opens A_2 while holding A_1 open, the light goes off. The question before us, then, is whether and, if so, what power can be assigned to Bailey in this situation.

Figure 4: Over-Power

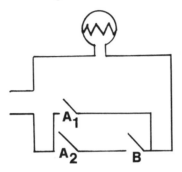

Arthur announces that on Monday one or both of his switches will be *fixed* for the whole day. To say that a switch is "fixed" is to say that its operator has put the switch into a given position and then has removed his hand and assumed a posture of rest with respect to its operation. There are a number of switch arrangements that might be considered. I shall deal with only four.

Arrangement I: Arthur fixes A_2 in the open position. On Monday Bailey is then bypassed as he was in the situation represented in Fig. 3. Bailey has no control. Arthur retains complete control via his other switch, A_1.

Arrangement II: Arthur fixes A_2 in the closed position. Since the flexible part of the circuit portrayed in Fig. 4 is now the parallel subcircuit governed by A_1 and B, it would seem reasonable to suppose that on Monday Bailey acquires the same complex of powers he has in the situation pictured in Fig. 1. Assuming that this is right, on Monday Bailey has full positive control and partial negative control with respect to E. This is because with A_2 fixed in closed position Bailey has power sufficient to effect E (by closing B) and he also has power so to act as to provide a necessary condition for not-E (B open). But, now, if we allow this, though nothing changes as regards Arthur's full positive control, what shall we say about Arthur's full negative control? Should we conclude that on Monday it is no longer his since on Monday Bailey has partial negative control? I think not. We have supposed that Arthur has closed A_2 and has assumed a posture of rest with respect to its operation. But this is not to suggest that he has left his station, paralyzed his hand, or in some other way lost his *ability* to operate A_2. By hypothesis, on Monday Arthur is keeping A_2 closed, but he *could* open it. He still has *power* sufficient to effect not-E. The right conclusion would thus appear to be that in this situation Arthur still has full negative control even though Bailey has acquired partial negative control. But, of course, this sounds paradoxical. It is to say that on Monday Arthur has power *sufficient* to effect not-E and yet that on Monday Bailey has power so to act as to provide a necessary condition for not-E. However, paradox does not really threaten. We can straighten it out if we make explicit a distinction which is already built into the situation. Bailey's partial negative control is *conditioned* in the sense that it is his only because and only as long as A_2 is fixed in the closed position. Arthur's full negative control is not conditioned in this sense. It is his whether or not any of the switches pictured in Fig. 4 are actually open or closed. The full description, then, is that on Monday Arthur has full *unconditional* negative control (as he always did) and on Monday Bailey has partial and *conditional* negative control with respect to E. We might put this so: on Monday, by closing A_2 and assuming a posture of rest with respect to its operation, Arthur *delegates* but does not thereby *lose* some negative control to Bailey. On Monday, *by Arthur's leave*, Bailey has partial negative control (and, for that matter, full positive control) with respect to E.

Arrangement III: Arthur fixes A_1 in the open position. In this circumstance the flexible part of the complex pictured in Fig. 4 is the series subcircuit governed by switches A_2 and B. We are thus prompted to say that on Monday Bailey acquires the cluster of powers he has in the circumstance represented in Fig. 2, viz., full negative control and partial positive control. But, again, the fact that Bailey has acquired partial positive control does not mean that Arthur has somehow lost full positive control. A_1 is open, but Arthur could easily close it. This is to say that Arthur has power that he is not exercising. Paradox? No. We can sort it out as we did above. Arthur's full positive control is unconditional, while Bailey's partial positive control (as well as his full negative control) is conditioned by the fact that Arthur is at rest with A_1 open. Bailey has been delegated power; by Arthur's leave Bailey has a say about whether the light goes on or off on Monday.

Arrangement IV: Arthur fixes A_2 in the closed position and A_1 in open position. Bailey now assumes full positive control and full negative control, i.e., complete control with respect to E. Of course, unlike Arthur's, Bailey's complete control is conditioned. It is his only because and only as long as Arthur chooses to keep things as they are. Still, Bailey's take-over is complete. For as long as Arthur is favorably disposed, it is Bailey who actually decides whether the light goes on or off.

With A_2 fixed in the closed position, with A_1 fixed in the open position, or with A_2 fixed in the closed position and A_1 fixed in the open position, Bailey has power. In each case his power is conditional, but it would not do to say that it is illusory or in any way less than real. In all three cases Bailey acquires the ability to make a causal contribution to the occurrence or non-occurrence of E. However, even in the case where both Arthur and Bailey have complete control with respect to E (arrangement IV), Arthur has a kind or dimension of control that Bailey does not have. In this situation, though both Arthur and Bailey have power sufficient to determine the condition *of the light*, Arthur has power sufficient to determine which, if any, powers Bailey shall have at any given moment. This last is what I am calling "over-power." It is the power one has when one can completely determine which, if any, powers are possessed by agents other than oneself.

II
Freedom within Omnipotence

Go back for a moment to the situation pictured in Fig. 3. Here Arthur has complete control with respect to E. But that is not all. In this circumstance Arthur not only has *power* sufficient to determine E and *power* sufficient to determine not-E, he *does in fact* determine E or he *does in fact* determine not-E. We might put this by saying that in the situation represented by Fig. 3 there is no *inefficacious position* for Arthur, i.e., there is no way to arrange things so that Arthur is not either effecting E or effecting not-E. Now, allowing "E" and "not-E" to take as values the occurrence or nonoccurrence respectively of any possible event, we emerge with Arthur as omnipotent. And what is interesting, I think, is that in this picture the omnipotent being is portrayed not only as one who has *power* to determine the occurrence or nonoccurrence of any possible event but as one who *does in fact* determine whatever it is in the universe that actually happens. This is the way in which John Calvin understood the notion of divine omnipotence. It is a view that allows for no significant distinction between the idea of omnipotence on the one hand and the idea of active, omni-determining providence on the other.[5] Further, and with this much established, if we include the actions of created beings among the events of the world, it is a concept of omnipotence that most would regard as quite incompatible with the idea of creaturely freedom. Here creatures not only do not control their own behavior, but that behavior is completely decided by the actions of the omni-determining being. All of this is quite explicit in Calvin. In fact, the last-mentioned implication is elaborated in his writings with great, indeed, bewilderingly abundant, enthusiasm.[6]

Move now to the situation diagramed in Fig. 4. Letting "E" and "not-E" take as values the occurrence and nonoccurrence respectively of any possible event, Arthur is again represented as an omnipotent being. But here we can make perfectly good sense of the idea that there are events that the omnipotent being neither determines to occur nor determines not to occur. In Fig. 4 there is an inefficacious position for Arthur, viz., one in which he has fixed A_1 in open position and A_2 in closed position. What this allows us to represent is what J. L. Mackie once aptly labeled "second-order omnipotence" — i.e., the power to determine that others shall determine some selection of worldly events.[7] This is what I am calling "over-power." But with this included as part of our notion of omnipotence, even if we allow the actions of finite agents to be numbered among the events of the world, there is no reason to deny that creatures have freedom in the theistic universe. All we need add is that their individual actions are among those events that the omnipotent being leaves for creatures to determine for themselves.

Urban and Walton tell us that if God has power sufficient to determine the occurrence or nonoccurrence of any possible event, then God "has all the power in the universe leaving no room for other centers of power." If God has complete control with respect to the occurrence of every possible event, then creatures have no control even with respect to their own behavior. But while there is a way of understanding the notion of omnipotence that does at least seem to deliver this conclusion (Calvin's), there is an alternative conception that seems equally clearly to avoid it. The latter trades on the possibility that God has power that he does not exercise but delegates to others to exercise instead. Calvin rejected this last mentioned thesis. He maintained that those who exploit it in their theological systems are "sophists" really committed to deny that God has complete control with respect to worldly events.[8] This is the contrapositive (and is thus the equivalent) of the reasoning employed by Urban and Walton as well as Flew and Griffin when deriving behavioral determinism from the doctrine of divine control. But the hiatus, I think, is manifest. As with one's power, one's control can extend further than one's actual determinations — as, for example, a government commission might have complete control over the price of gasoline and yet be content (for as long as they cooperate) to let individual oil companies set the actual price per gallon. The key, I think, lies in the notion of over-power. If it is coherent (as I think it is), there can be creaturely freedom within the scope of divine omnipotence.

III
St. Thomas on Free Will and Evil

In pt. 1-2, q. 79, a. 1 of the *Summa theologiae* St. Thomas Aquinas addresses the question of whether God is the cause of sin. Most of his response to this enquiry is contained in the following excerpt:[9]

> I answer that man is, in two ways, a cause either of his own or of another's sin. First, directly, namely by inclining his or another's

will to sin; secondly, indirectly, namely by not preventing someone from sinning. . . . Now God cannot be directly the cause of sin, either in Himself or in another, since every sin is a departure from the order, which is to God as the end: whereas God inclines and turns all things to Himself as to their last end . . . so that it is impossible that He should be either to Himself or to another the cause of departing from the order which is to Himself. Therefore He cannot be directly the cause of sin. In like manner neither can He cause sin indirectly. For it happens that God does not give some the assistance were He to give, they would not sin. But He does all this according to the order of His Wisdom and Justice: so that if someone sins it is not imputable to Him as though He were the cause of that sin; even as the pilot is not said to cause the wrecking of the ship, through not steering the ship, unless he ceases to steer while able and bound to steer. It is therefore evident that God is nowise a cause of sin.

But it might be objected (obj. 3):

The cause of the cause is the cause of the effect. Now God is the cause of free-will, which itself is the cause of sin. Therefore God is the cause of sin.

To this St. Thomas replies:

The effect which proceeds from the middle cause, according as it is subordinate to the first cause, is reduced to that first cause: but if it proceed from the middle cause, according as it operates outside of the order of the first cause, it is not reduced to that first cause: thus if a servant do anything contrary to his master's orders, it is not ascribed to the master as though he were the cause thereof. In like manner sin, which the free-will commits against the commandment of God, is not attributed to God as being the cause.

Before proceeding, I should like to identify what I take to be the essentials of the reasoning advanced in these several passages.

Verbally, the generative question concerns the *causes* of sin. But on the interpretation that I shall assume (and, let me agree, there might be others), the real issue has less to do with establishing causes than it has with locating *responsibility*. St. Thomas assures us that although the universe contains creatures who sometimes do what is wrong, God is "nowise the cause" of this behavior. The point (I shall assume) is that this behavior is not (as he says) "imputable" to God in the sense that God is not to be held responsible for it. The argument for this conclusion can perhaps best be seen as unfolding in two broad steps:

(1) God created beings with free will, i.e., (as St. Thomas says in *Summa theologiae,* pt. 1, q. 83) "the power to choose." (This, of course, is an exercise of over-power on God's part.) But if creatures have the power to choose, they are then able to opt for courses of action that are forbidden by divine command. Assume that they do. These, then, are cases in which the "middle cause" (free will) is operating "outside of the order of the first cause" (contrary to God's command) and thus, although the first cause (God) is indeed the cause (creator) of the middle cause, he cannot be said to be the cause — i.e., responsible for — the final effect, sin. Thomas points out that if the servant acts contrary to his master's commands, the actions of the servant cannot be "ascribed" to the master. The master, in other words, cannot be held responsible for them.

(2) But, it might be wondered, could not God step in and prevent his creatures from acting contrary to his orders? St. Thomas says that he could — he might offer what Thomas calls "assistance." But in his wisdom and justice God often does not provide such assistance. Still he is not responsible for the sins committed. Since creatures have been given control over their own behavior, they alone must shoulder responsibility for what they do. Thomas says that God is like the pilot of a ship that is wrecked at a time when he is not steering. He cannot be held responsible for the wreck unless it can be shown that he was both able and bound to steer. If we think of the actions of a created agent as movements of a ship under the control of an ordinary seaman rather than the pilot, then Thomas's position is that God is able to steer — through "assistance." The conclusion must be that since created agents have been given control, God is under no obligation to steer.

There is one feature of the reasoning just reviewed that seems to me to be especially insightful. I think I can best get at it by comparing St. Thomas's theodicy with the one that Alvin Plantinga has recently tried to establish as possibly true, i.e., free of contradiction, but does not himself claim to be actually correct. I'll pause for a moment to sketch the highlights of Plantinga's thinking.[10]

God can create a world in which creatures perform morally right actions only if he creates agents with free will. Unless it is performed freely, an action has no moral value (positive or negative) and thus does not qualify as morally right. But if God creates agents with free will, he then provides the precondition for wrongdoing as well as rightdoing. And (the argument continues) God cannot provide the precondition for wrongdoing and, at the same time, prevent wrong actions from being performed. Now assume that no matter which free creatures God might create, all would opt to perform at least some immoral actions. (This last is claimed to be consistent whether or not it is actually true.) It is then not within God's power to create a world in which creatures perform morally right actions but do not also perform some actions that are wrong. God is justified in creating the present world — one containing free creatures who perform both right actions and wrong actions — because in this world there is a favorable "balance" of right action over wrong. (That there is such a balance is the second point that is claimed to be consistent but is not advanced as an actual truth.)

This argument shares two things in common with St. Thomas's: first, its premise-set includes essential mention of creaturely free will; and, second, at bottom, it reaches the conclusion that apart from the act whereby God confers free will on creatures in the first place, God is not responsible and thus cannot be blamed for the fact that creaturess perform immoral actions. However in this theodicy the last-mentioned conclusion is reached a little differently than it is by St. Thomas. Plantinga says that as long as men are free to perform morally right actions, not even an omnipotent being can prevent them from performing morally wrong actions. In his words: "(God) can forestall the occurrence of moral evil only by removing the possibility of moral good," i.e., only by removing free will.[11] This (presumably) logical limitation on God's power is what supports — indeed, *requires* — the conclusion that apart from having provided free will in the first place, God cannot be held responsible for wrong actions. Nothing like this can be found in the passages cited above from St. Thomas. In fact, Thomas claims that although men have free will, it is within God's power to provide what he calls "assistance" in cases where men would otherwise do what is wrong: by way of "assistance" God could ensure that no creature performs an immoral action. But, it will be objected, to "assist" creatures in the way indicated would be to *cause* them not to behave in morally objectionable ways. This, in turn, would be to deprive creatures of free will and thus to preclude, not only wrong action, but the very possibility of right action as well. This objection seems clearly to turn on a mistake. Suppose that God were to provide "assistance" only when needed. At best what follows is that men would not be free to perform a specific range of actions, viz., wrong actions. But this no more implies the absence of free will than does, e.g., the fact that men are not now free to hang unsupported in the atmosphere or to travel faster than the speed of light. One has free will if one is free to choose between alternatives. But this does not require that the alternatives in question be unlimited. I lock my car or leave my phone off the hook. This limits my neighbor's alternatives, but it does not thereby reduce the number of free agents in the world. If God were to provide "assistance" in cases where men would otherwise do what is wrong, this would diminish men's options but would in no way diminish the free population. The men "assisted" would still be free to choose among a myriad of nonwrong actions. Most importantly, the men "assisted" would still be free to perform those actions that are morally right. Analogy: The police in Sunnyville have developed a system whereby they can anticipate and prevent all instances of illegal behavior. Their techniques are action-specific, i.e., they do not employ massive prevention measures such as imprisoning the whole population or even potential lawbreakers. Citizens are free to do as they please as long as they do not attempt to break the law. Only illegal behavior is prevented — it is stopped before it can be successfully completed. It is perhaps not irrelevant to add that Sunnyville is filled with citizens of all ages who have won special awards for meritorious behavior. So far as I can see, an omnipotent (add omniscient) being could prevent wrong action while at the same time allowing creatures free will and thus preserving the precondition of morally right action. Since the theodicy that Plantinga discusses depends importantly on his insistence to the contrary, that theodicy seems to me to be conceptually deficient.[12] However, in the present context the point to be emphasized has less to do with Plantinga's reasoning than it does with the theory advanced by St. Thomas. Whatever may be our final verdict regarding the success of Thomas's theodicy, I think he was right to acknowledge at the outset that God can prevent creatures — even free creatures — from sinning. It is to his credit that he faced up squarely to this implication of traditional thinking about God's capabilities. I turn now to probe the rest of his thinking on this topic.

Making use of an example that is inspired by St. Thomas's analogy of the pilot, I want first to consider two fanciful situations designed to flex part of the complex web of ordinary intuitions that govern our thinking on the topic of moral responsibility. The example I have in mind is that of the automobile used in driver-training programs which is equipped with what is called "dual control." In addition to the usual controls operated from the driver's side, vehicles with dual control are rigged with a functional brake peddle on the floor of the passenger's side as well as with a second ignition switch by which the in-car instructor can cut the engine at will. More sophisticated models include a steering wheel on the passenger's side. We could easily imagine an arrangement that would completely replicate the situation diagramed in Fig. 4 — two full sets of controls and a switch similar to A_2 by which the instructor can engage or disengage the control system operated by the trainee. The cases I want to consider are these:

Case I: An intersection, plainly marked with a legal stop sign, is located on a practice track operated by the City of San Diego as part of its driver-training program. Though the track is large and encompasses a variety of cross streets, bridges, etc., for safety reasons only one car at a time is allowed to run. Bailey (the trainee) is driving; he has been thoroughly briefed as regards traffic regulations. Arthur (the instructor) is in the passenger seat with his special ignition switch in "on" position. He has assumed a posture of watchful rest with respect to the operation of the car. As Bailey approaches the intersection of interest, he accelerates beyond the legal speed limit. The car runs the stop sign and continues through the intersection without so much as the slightest hesitation. Throughout Arthur makes no move to interfere. At the end of the run Bailey is chastised for his errors and is given a failing grade on his performance for the day.

Assuming that there are no extenuating circumstances (e.g., that Bailey did not suffer an attack of narcolepsy while at the wheel), I think it is clear that Bailey is responsible for the fact that the car was traveling in excess of the speed limit and failed to stop at the intersection as required. He was cognizant, informed, and was driving the car. He was thus justly chastised and punished (in the form of the failing score) for his performance. But what about Arthur? To be sure, Bailey was driving, but Arthur could have prevented the violations. He could have hit the brake, cut the engine, or both. Maybe Arthur should be chastised and punished as well. Maybe Arthur should be chastised and punished *instead.*

Note, first of all, that were we simply interested in locating *responsibility*, the honors would probably have to be split between the two principals. With respect to the fact that the car was traveling in excess of the speed limit and failed to stop at the intersection, Bailey is responsible as doer and Arthur is responsible as permitter. Nor is this paradoxical or odd. It is a standard way of distributing responsibility both in ordinary moral contexts and in legal settings as well.[13] However, the question before us concerns *blame* and not just responsibility. And on this issue I think that Bailey alone must accept the burden. Arthur is not to be chastised or punished. In fact, he might even be praised for his restraint and rewarded (in the form of a raise) for his patience as an instructor. After all, how is Bailey going to learn how to drive if he is never permitted to make a mistake?

Case II: An intersection again plainly marked with a legal stop sign is located in downtown San Diego. The time is evening rush hour, and the intersection is crowded with vehicles and pedestrians. Bailey is driving, and as he approaches the scene, he accelerates beyond the legal speed limit and, narrowly missing the stop sign itself, careens into the busy cross street. The car hits a loaded school bus which was fully visible from the beginning and clearly had the right of way. As before, Arthur makes no effort to interfere. In the end six children are taken to the emergency ward with broken bones and bleeding wounds. Two are dead before morning.

Again, assuming that there are no extenuating circumstances, Bailey must be assigned responsibility for the violations and the consequent tragedy. He could not plead incapacity, and he was surely aware of the danger inherent in his illegal action. Blame and punishment would be fully appropriate. But what about Arthur? As in case I, he can again be assigned responsibility—the responsibility that goes with his role as permitter. But this time the circumstances clearly indicate that he may not be just responsible, but *liable.* Look at it this way: Bailey was a trainee—inexperienced, nervous from the outset. One could expect that the prospect of negotiating a busy intersection would occasion some degree of panic. However, Arthur was the instructor—experienced and confident as a driver. Further, we might imagine that Arthur had been over the route many times with dozens of trainees. He should have anticipated the problem and been ready to act as soon as disaster began to unfold. To be sure, Bailey did it—he ran the stop sign, hit the bus, and killed the children. But the point is that although he had operational control of the vehicle, he should not have had it—Arthur should have had it. Arthur had over-power. Unless there is something in the story that we have not yet been told, it would appear that it was his obligation to take control from Bailey and guide the car himself.

In the example just sketched I have assumed that Arthur has complete control with respect to the motions of the car but not that he has complete control (or even partial control) with respect to Bailey's bodily activities, decisions, or choices. Arthur is thus responsible for the motion of the car (and its consequences), but that is as far as his responsibility extends. However, in the case of God the range of control broadens. Allowing that the activities (even deciding or choosing activities) of creatures can be included in the class of events, God has complete control not only with respect to the circumstances that result from the freely chosen actions of creatures but with respect to the freely chosen actions themselves. Now St. Thomas maintains that since creatures have been given free will and can thus be held responsible for their actions generally and for those that are contrary to divine command in particular, God is "nowise the cause," i.e., is responsible neither for the actions nor (presumably) for the events that issue therefrom. I think that this is a mistake even in the case where the actions of creatures have no morally relevant dimension other than the fact that they violate law. In case I, for example, Authur is responsible *qua* permitter for the fact that the car is traveling in excess of the speed limit and fails to stop at the intersection as required. In this case it is blame and not responsibility that is justly assigned to Bailey alone. Thinking of the actions of creatures as analogous to the motions of the car, even if it could be argued that God is not to be blamed for creaturely behavior that is contrary to law, that he is *responsible* for such behavior seems to me to be clear. However, where the reasoning involved in St. Thomas's theodicy goes wrong in a really salient way is where it is applied to cases in which the actions of creatures not only are contrary to divine command but result in the suffering and misery of other sentient beings. Here I might point to dramatic cases such as Auschwitz and Bangladesh — holocausts consequent on immoral actions of overwhelming magnitude. But perhaps in the long run it is the everyday tragedies that issue from commonplace offenses that are better used for illustration. It is when the girl next door is raped and strangled that attention is more likely to be peaked. Working St. Thomas's example of the disobedient servant together with that of the pilot, these are cases in which the ordinary seaman who is left to steer not only disobeys the pilot's orders but wrecks the ship and drowns his shipmates as well. Assume now that God not only has over-power with respect to human actions but, being omniscient, also knows in advance that his commands will be violated and that suffering will be the result. The full analogy, then, is the pilot who is not only able to take over the wheel but is fully aware that if he fails to do so, his orders will be disobeyed and disaster will strike. Shall we say that since the seaman who has been given control violates command, he is responsible and appropriately blamed for the wreck? That seems right. What would be wrong, however, is from this to conclude that in the situation imagined the pilot's responsibility ceased when he delegated control and thus that he is not *also* responsible for the ensuing wreck. And, of course, it is the counterpart of this that constitutes the thrust of St. Thomas's theodicy. It is the claim that since creatures have been given control over their own behavior and are thus responsible for their own immoral actions, apart from the act whereby he conferred free will in the first place (which is not here at issue), God is simply not called upon to answer. But if God has over-power, this thesis is simplistic to the point of being absurd. As long as he retains control over their powers to control their individual actions, God is not just responsible for the fact that creatures *can* sin (i.e., that they have free will), he *as well as they* is responsible for what they *actually do*.

Epilogue: So how shall God answer — or, better, how shall we answer for him? Note that this question becomes relevant only after we agree that the conclusion reached in St. Thomas's theodicy is false. Insofar as God is not responsible, to that extent is justification neither required nor even appropriate. But, again, how shall we answer? What is needed is easily described but may be difficult to deliver. It is a reason for thinking that when shipwreck is pending, God is not (though quite able), *himself*, "bound to steer."

IV
Augustine on Evil

In chapter 96 of the *Enchiridion* St. Augustine writes as follows concerning the existence of evil in the theistic universe:[14]

Nor can we doubt that God does well even in the permission of what is evil. For He permits it only in the justice of His judgment. And surely all that is just and good. Although, therefore, evil, in so far as it is evil, is not a good, yet the fact that evil as well as good exists, is a good. For if it were not a good that evil exists, its existence would not be permitted by the omnipotent God, who without doubt can as easily refuse to permit what He does not wish, as bring about what He does wish. And if we do not believe this, the very first sentence of our creed is endangered, wherein we profess to believe in God the Father Almighty. For He is not truly called Almighty if He cannot do whatever He pleases, or if the power of His almighty will is hindered by the will of any creature whatsoever.

In chapter 100 of the same text the principle enunciated in the foregoing passage is applied to the special case of immoral action:

These are the great works of the Lord, sought out according to all His pleasure, and so wisely sought out, that when the intelligent creation, both angelic and human, sinned, doing not His will but their own, He used the very will of the creature which was working in opposition to the Creator's will as an instrument for carrying out His will, the Supremely Good thus turning to good account even what is evil. . . . For as far as relates to their own consciousness, these creatures did what God wished not to be done; but in view of God's omnipotence, they could in nowise effect their purpose. For in the very fact that they acted in opposition to His will, His will concerning them was fulfilled. And hence it is that "the works of the Lord are great, sought out according to all His pleasure," because in a way unspeakably strange and wonderful, even what is done in opposition to His will does not defeat His will. For it would not be done did He not permit it (and of course His permission is not unwilling, but willing): nor would a Good Being permit evil to be done only that in His omnipotence He can turn evil into good.

Augustine says that if a man sins, he does so by God's leave and with his permission. Since God is omnipotent and could thus readily prevent it, if he did not permit it, the man simply would not succeed in sinning. Shall we then conclude that God is to be blamed for immoral actions and the shipwrecks such as Auschwitz that follow as consequences? Of course Augustine's answer is negative. He claims that "in a way unspeakably strange and wonderful" these very evils are turned to good account. In the final analysis, whatever evils God permits (including sinful actions) make a positive contribution to the ultimate good. If they did not, God, being perfectly good as well as omnipotent, simply would not allow them to occur.

This theodicy stands in contrast to the one offered by St. Thomas (as well as the one discussed by Alvin Plantinga) in at least two important ways.

First, the hinge of St. Thomas's reasoning consists in the claim that since creatures are free to either obey or disobey divine command, if they choose not to do so, they alone can be held responsible (and thus properly blamed) for their immoral actions and their untoward consequences. But this is not Augustine's view — at least not in the passages we are now considering. Here the focus of the thinking has nothing to do with the assignment of responsibility. It consists, instead, in Augustine's evaluation of the permitted evils. The crucial claim is that immoral actions and their consequent outcomes have positive value by virtue of their contribution to the ultimate good. It is because of this, and not because he lacks responsibility for the events in question, that God is not to be blamed for their occurrence. Blame is appropriate only in cases where what is permitted has negative value. Thus, if we agree with Augustine that "the fact that evil as well as good exists is a good," to blame

God for allowing evil would make no sense at all. The situation here is reminiscent of the practice-track situation where the chain between the traffic violations and Arthur's culpability is broken not at the link of responsibility but at the next one down, viz., blame.

Second, St. Thomas's theodicy has as an essential ingredient the claim that creatures have free will. It is because of this that creatures, rather than God, are responsible for their immoral actions and the events that result. But Augustine's theodicy requires no such premise. Since the argument is not aimed at shifting responsibility away from God, it could proceed as well even if it were admitted that God *alone* is responsible for what happens, i.e., that creatures (to turn things around) are "nowise the cause." Note, I am not here suggesting that Augustine actually held this view: I suspect that if he had, it would have caused trouble elsewhere in his theology. Note, too, that Augustine's theodicy in no way precludes a doctrine of creaturely freedom and a consequent acknowledgment of creaturely responsibility. The point I am after is that as it stands and is considered apart from other elements of his theology, Augustine's theodicy is independent of any assumption concerning the existence or nonexistence of creaturely freedom. This again marks a difference between his and St. Thomas's theodicy. It also provides occasion for an interesting historical observation, viz., that in bk. 1, ch. 28, sec. 3, of the *Institutes*, Calvin cites with profound approval most of the second passage from the *Enchiridion* quoted at the beginning of this section.[15] Calvin apparently saw very clearly that unlike the one advanced by St. Thomas, Augustine's theodicy could be consistently adopted in a theological system in which it is also held that God alone determines whatever happens in the universe, including the actions of creatures.

I have argued that if we think of God as having over-power, the doctrine of divine omnipotence does not conflict with the notion of creaturely freedom. I have also argued that this same assumption requires the rejection of any theodicy in which it is claimed that apart from the act whereby God confers free will to creatures in the first place, God is not responsible for the evil in the universe that consists in or results from the immoral actions of creatures. On the basis of the admittedly sketchy remarks in this last section, I now want to add that even if theodicies of this last-mentioned sort are discarded, Augustine's remains to be considered. The argument that touches the former does nothing to undermine the cogency of the latter. Further, although Augustine's stance on the problem of evil is bold, I am inclined to think that it can be formulated in a way that avoids conceptual incoherence.[16] With patient attention to the problem of identifying the good to which permitted evils ultimately contribute, it may also be capable of more specific development than Augustine himself ever attempted.[17] But whether or not either of these last speculations is right, if God has over-power, at least one negative conclusion seems to me to be in order. If there is promise of adequate theodicy sometime in the future, it does not lie in some further effort to establish that God is not responsible for the freely performed, immoral actions of creatures.

NOTES

1. Linwood Urban and Douglas Walton, eds., *The Power of God: Readings on Omnipotence and Evil* (New York: Oxford University Press, 1978), pp. 192-93.

2. Anthony Flew, *God and Philosophy* (New York: Harcourt, Brace and World, 1966), pp. 46-47.

3. Ibid., pp. 55-56.

4. David Griffin, *God, Power and Evil: A Process Theodicy* (Philadelphia: Westminster Press, 1976), chs. 17-18. See also Charles Hartshorne's article "Omnipotence," in *An Encyclopedia of Religion*, ed. Vergilius Fern (New York: Philosophical Library, 1945), and ch. 2 of *The Divine Relativity* (New Haven: Yale University Press, 1938).

5. John Calvin, *Institutes of the Christian Religion*, bk. 1, ch. 16, secs. 3-4.

6. For example, see ibid., bk. 2, chs. 1-5, and bk. 3, chs. 21-23.

7. J. L. Mackie, "Evil and Omnipotence," *Mind* 64 (1955): 200-12. See also the third paragraph of Peter Geach's essay "Omnipotence," *Philosophy* 48 (1973): 7-20, where he briefly describes what he calls God's "Almightiness" or "power over all things." Incidentally, I shall not here deal with Mackie's claim that a single being cannot have unlimited first-order omnipotence and unlimited second-order omnipotence (power to determine the power of others) at the same time. For

what I think is the correct reply to Mackie on this point, see Bernard Mayo's "Mr. Keene on Omnipotence," *Mind* 70 (1961): 249-50.

8. John Calvin, *Institutes of the Christian Religion*, bk. 1, ch. 16, secs. 3-4. In section 4 Calvin writes: "Not so gross is the error of those who attribute governance to God but of a confused and mixed sort, as I have said, namely, one that by a general motion resolves and drives the system of the universe, with its several parts, but which does not specifically direct the action of individual creatures. Yet this error, also, is not tolerable; for by this providence which they call universal, they teach that nothing hinders all creatures from being contingently moved, or man from turning himself hither and thither by the free choice of his will. (This view, Calvin continues, takes from God) the chief thing: that he directs everything by his incomprehensible wisdom and disposes it to his own end. And so in name only, not in fact, it makes God the ruler of the universe because it deprives him of his control. What, I pray you, is it to have control but so to be in authority that you rule in a determined order those things over which you are placed?"

9. The following passages are literally translated by Fathers of the English Dominican Province (New York: Benziger Bros., 1947).

10. The following paragraph contains a summary of the argument developed by Alvin Plantinga in the first ten sections of *God, Freedom and Evil* (New York: Harper Torchbooks, Harper & Row, 1974), sec. A. Plantinga supplies his own sketch of the argument on pp. 30-31.

11. Plantinga, *God, Freedom and Evil*, p. 30. The whole passage reads as follows:

> To create creatures capable of moral good . . . (God) must create creatures capable of moral evil; and he can't give these creatures the freedom to perform moral evil and at the same time prevent them from doing so. As it turns out, sadly enough, some of the free creatures God created went wrong in the exercise of their freedom; this is the source of moral evil. The fact that free creatures sometimes go wrong, however, counts neither against God's omnipotence nor against His goodness; for he could have forestalled the occurrence of moral evil only by removing the possibility of moral good.

The conclusion is, then, that although God is omnipotent, he *could not* create a world in which creatures perform right actions (which requires free will) without creating a world in which creatures also perform immoral actions. Plantinga adds that the "heart" of his own position (formulated in what he calls the "Free Will Defense") is that this conclusion is "possible," i.e., free of contradiction.

12. I developed this point a little differently in an earlier article entitled "Plantinga on Free Will and Evil," *Religious Studies* 15 (1979): sec. 5, pp. 470-72.

13. As regards the latter, the idea that there is permitter as well as doer responsibility is the major ingredient in the principle of *respondeat superior* ("let the master answer"), which affirms, in effect, that a person is responsible for the actions of others who are (or who ought to be) under that person's control, e.g., one's employees. See any good legal dictionary under the heading of "agency."

14. These passages are taken from vol. 1 of *The Basic Writings of Augustine*, ed. W. J. Oats, trans. J. F. Shaw (New York: Random House, 1948).

15. See also Calvin's *Institutes*, bk. 1, ch. 17 secs. 5 and 11.

16. See sec. 2 of Nelson Pike, "Hume on Evil," *Philosophical Review* 72 (1963): 180-97. See especially Roderick Chisholm's splendid development of this idea in "The Defeat of Good and Evil," *Proceedings of The American Philosophical Association* 42 (1968-69): 21-38.

17. What has come to be known as the "soul-making" theodicy specifies the ultimate good as (what might be called) "spiritual maturity," which includes certain virtuous dispositions as forebearance and steadfastness. The argument is that evil in the world is logically indispensable for the ultimate good. In effect, the soul-making theodicy asks us to think of the world as a kind of training grounds—a practice track of the sort described in Case I above. On this view Case II is then not really different from Case I. God permits both the legal violations and their consequences because they are required as part of the soul-making process. I think one can see in this a more specific version of the sort of reasoning Augustine introduces. And while I do not care to claim that it is actually successful, it does suggest that Augustine's theodicy may be capable of more concrete development. For details on the soul-making theodicy see John Hick, *Evil and the God of Love* (New York: Harper and Row, 1966), parts 3 and 4. See also Clement Dore's "An Examination of the 'Soul-Making' Theodicy," *American Philosophical Quarterly* 7 (1970): 119-30.

A Theodicy of Heaven and Hell*

RICHARD SWINBURNE

I

Most theistic religions have a doctrine of the afterlife in which the eternal fate of a man depends on how he has led his life on earth. A doctrine of traditional Christianity, as of some other theistic religions, is that the good go to heaven and the bad are permanently barred from heaven. Christians dispute about whether there are intermediate groups who have intermediate fates (e.g., whether unbaptized babies go to limbo or the imperfectly good have to go to purgatory before they get to heaven). But I shall avoid these issues in order to consider only the ultimate fate of the clearly good and the clearly bad. I wish to investigate whether the permanent separation of the good and bad is consonant with the supposed goodness of God. Philosophers have devoted a lot of attention to considering whether it is coherent to suppose that there can be an afterlife, but very little to considering the morality of the supposed division between the sheep and the goats.

In traditional Catholic orthodoxy heaven is for those who have faith formed by love (*caritas*). Faith was understood in the Catholic tradition between Aquinas and the First Vatican Council as "belief." Aquinas echoed Hugh of St. Victor's definition of faith as something midway between knowledge (*scientia*)

---

*This paper is based on material used in my book *Faith and Reason* (Oxford, 1981). It is printed here by kind permission of the publisher, Oxford University Press.

and conjecture (*opinio*)[1] — i.e., belief. To have love it is normally necessary to do works of love — though a man totally ready to do such works but dying before having an opportunity to do them also would seem to have charity. One obvious work to which faith would give rise would be to seek from God the forgiveness of sins and baptism, and thereafter to live the Christian way within the church. Despite much sound and fury during the Reformation about men being saved "by faith alone," I do not think that Protestant doctrine on this matter was in any significant way different from the official Catholic doctrine (though it was different from popular misrepresentations of Catholic doctrine).[2] For the Protestants understood "faith" as more than mere belief, as involving also trust in God and giving rise in appropriate circumstances to good works. So on both views you need belief and a readiness to act in the right way (good will) in order to go to heaven.

Yet why should God insist either on right belief or on good will as an entry condition for heaven? To start with, what is the justice in someone losing his eternal salvation merely for having the wrong beliefs? After all, he may never have heard of the Christian Gospel, or if he has, he may never have heard of good reason for believing it. In my view belief is passive. We cannot choose our beliefs; we can only force a change over time by nonrational means or pursue honest investigation and allow ourselves to conform to the beliefs which that investigation suggests. Even if you hold, as Aquinas did, that a man can to some extent choose his beliefs, the only honest thing to do is to hold those beliefs which the evidence best supports, as Aquinas also held.[3] So what is the justice in punishing the man who disbelieves, despite sincere inquiry into the relative merits of such religions as he is acquainted with? Surely all honest inquirers with sufficient love ought to go to heaven.

Most Christians today, I think, hold that God takes such honest inquirers to heaven. That he would do so was proclaimed as official Catholic doctrine by the Second Vatican Council. The latter declared that all men who strive to live a good life and who through no fault of their own "do not know the Gospel of Christ and his Church . . . . can attain to everlasting salvation." This possibility is open not only to theists but even to those who, through no fault of their own, "have not yet arrived at an explicit knowledge of God."[4] This was, I believe, a claim made in effect also by many earlier theologians and implicit in the gospel itself.[5] What matters is that people shall honestly seek after the truth, but if they do not find the truth (i.e., the Christian faith) in this life, that shall not debar them from heaven. However, if you can get to heaven without having true religious beliefs, why does it matter so much that people shall honestly seek after such beliefs? And the question remains: Why are the men of bad will excluded from heaven? Would not a generous God give the joys of heaven to good and bad alike? Or at any rate mold the bad to become good so as to gain heaven? Or at least give them a second chance? What is the justice of a man's fate being sealed at death?

There have been in our century many Christians worried by this latest difficulty who have adopted a universalist account of the afterlife: all men go to heaven sooner or later.[6] However it seems to me that such a doctrine is not that of the New Testament, and that those who espouse it have not taken into account some important points about the nature of human happiness and human choice which support a more traditional doctrine.

Before we can ask why certain people should not go to heaven and why true belief matters, we need to ask what heaven is and why certain people should go to heaven.

II

Heaven is a place where people enjoy eternally a supremely worthwhile happiness. But what is that, and why are the traditional occupations of heaven likely to provide it?

Happiness is not basically a matter of having pleasant sensations. Certainly it involves the absence of unpleasant sensations and may be found in having pleasant sensations, but this is not its essence. There are no pleasant sensations had by the man who is happy in reading a good book or playing a round of golf with a friend, or by a man who is happy because his son is making a success of the business which the father founded. Basically a man's happiness consists in doing what he wants to be doing and having happen what he wants to have happen. The man who is happy playing golf is happy because he is doing what he wants to be doing. Someone who is having pleasant sensations may indeed be happy for that reason, but he will not be happy if he does not want to have these sensations, e.g., if he wants to try and do without such things for a period.

Unfortunately men so often have conflicting wants, e.g., wants to have the pleasurable sensations caused by heroin and wants to avoid heroin addiction. Sometimes these conflicts are explicitly acknowledged; sometimes they are ones of which we are only half-conscious; and sometimes they are suppressed from consciousness altogether. A man will only be fully happy if he has no conflicting wants; if he is doing what he wants to be doing and wants in no way to be doing anything else. A man who does have conflicting wants may nevertheless still be on balance happy — especially if he is doing what he really thinks to be most worthwhile.

However, although someone may be fully happy doing some action or having something happen, this happiness may arise from a false factual belief or from doing an action or being in a situation which, objectively, is not really a very good one. Happiness is surely more to be prized according as the happy man has true beliefs about what is happening and according as what is happening is in fact of great value or only of little value. A man who is happy because he believes that his son is making a success of the business, when in fact he is not, has a happiness which is not as worth having as the happiness of the man who has a true belief that his son is making a success of the business. We can see this by asking ourselves which we would choose if faced with a choice of much happiness with a false belief that something marvellous was so, or small happiness with a true belief that some small good thing was so. Further, a man who is happy because he is watching a pornographic film by himself, or because he has made men sneer at some companion, has a happiness which is less to be prized than the happiness of a man enjoying a drink in company or watching the performance of a great work of art. That this is so can be seen by those of us capable of enjoying all such pleasures, comparing them for their worth. Insofar as happiness is to be prized, I shall call it deep, and I shall contrast deep happiness with shallow happiness which is to be prized less.

It follows that a man's deepest happiness is to be found in pursuing successfully a task of supreme value and being in a situation of supreme value, when he has true beliefs about this and wants to be only in that situation doing those actions. What are the most worthwhile actions, the most worthwhile tasks to pursue? I suggest that they are developing our understanding of the world and beautifying it, developing our friendship with others, and helping others toward a deeply happy life. And what are the most worthwhile situations? The having of pleasurable sensations is desirable, but they are the better for coming from the doing of worthwhile actions. People want the sensations of sexual pleasure through the development of a personal relationship, not by themselves. It is better to drink alcohol in company than alone. And so on. And a worthwhile situation will be one in which the good triumphs in the world, and one's own contribution toward this is recognized.

If all this is correct, the occupations of the inhabitants of the heaven depicted by traditional Christian theologians would be supremely worthwhile, and so would their situation be. If the world depends for its being on God, a personal ground of being, the fullest development of understanding will be growth in the understanding of the nature of God himself. Friendship is of great value to a man when his friends are good people, who take an interest in him and are enjoyable company in virtue of their kindness and ability to keep him interested. Friendship with God would be of supreme value, for he is (by definition) perfectly good and, being (by definition) omnipotent and omniscient, will ever be able to hold our interest by showing us new facets of reality and above all his own nature. According to Christian theology God takes an interest in his creatures and exercises that ability to show us ever-new facets of reality. The principal occupation of heaven is the enjoyment of the friendship of God. This has been traditionally described as the "Beatific Vision" of God. Aquinas stresses that this "vision" is an act of ours, not merely something that happens to us.[7] Knowledge in heaven will be more sure than on earth. On earth people depend on sense organs and nervous systems that may lead them astray or let them down. Christian theology assures people of a more direct grasp on reality in the hereafter. God will be present to the inhabitants of heaven as intimately as their own thoughts. Friendship with persons involves acknowledgment of their worth. So friendship with God, the supremely good source of being, involves adoration and worship.[8] According to Christian tradition heaven will also comprise friendship with good finite beings,[9] including those who have been our companions on earth. The task of comprehending and worshipping God will be a cooperative one, one in cooperation with those who have shared a man's lesser tasks on earth. Christian theology has always stressed both that heaven will include a renewal of earthly acquaintance and also that the enjoyment of such acquaintance will not be its main point. And, of course, one always enjoys acquaintance the better if it serves some further point, if one and one's fellows are working together to attain a goal. Even friendship with God would involve his helping us toward understanding himself and fulfilling other heavenly tasks. The main other such task, according to traditional theology, is helping others toward their deepest happiness (and perhaps also beautifying the world). According to Christian tradition the saints have work to do (by intercession or other means[10]) in bringing others into the sphere of God's love. These others may be like many on earth, half-developed beings ignorant of their capacities for these tasks, with wounds of body and soul to be healed. But the relation of those in heaven to those others will be of a different kind from the bodily relation which we have to our fellows on earth. A man seeks friendship with others not only for his own sake but for theirs, as part of helping others toward a deeply happy life. The most worthwhile such helping would be helping others toward their own deepest happiness, and thus seeking this sort of friendship also indirectly contributes to the seeker's own happiness.

I suspect that only that sort of life would be worth living forever. Only a task which made continued progress valuable for its own sake but which would take an infinite time to finish would be worth doing forever; only a situation which would be evermore worth having would be worth living in for ever. The growing development of a friendship with God who (if he is the sort of God pictured by Christian theology) has ever-new aspects of himself to reveal, and the bringing of others into an ever-developing relationship with God, would provide a life worth living for ever. A man who desired only to do the good (and had a right idea of what was good) would want that sort of life for ever. Most earthly occupations indeed pall after a time, but the reason why they pall is that there are no new facets to them which a man wants to have. And also most earthly occupations are rightly judged only to be worth a finite amount of interest, because there are not ever-new facets to them which are greatly worthwhile having. A man who has molded his desires so as to seek only the good and its continuation would not, given the Christian doctrine of God, be bored in eternity.[11]

A man in heaven would be in a situation of supreme value, for his own worth (such as it is) will be acknowledged, and the good there will be triumphing. Further, traditionally, people will get bodily pleasure out of being in heaven. Aquinas[12] quotes Augustine[13] as saying that blessedness involves "joy in the truth" and that the happiness of heaven will involve the body.[14] Aquinas taught that man's ultimate goal is *beatitudo*, literally "blessedness" but often translated "happiness." This translation is a bad one. The English word "happiness" denotes a subjective state, a man doing and having done to him what he wants—even if what he is doing is not of great worth and he has false beliefs about what is going on. I argued that happiness is most worth having when the agent has true beliefs about his condition and gets his happiness from doing what is worthwhile. It is such worthwhile happiness which is *beatitudo*.[15] The inhabitants of a Christian heaven will be performing actions of supreme worth and be in a situation of supreme worth, and they will know that they are doing such actions and in such a situation. Hence they will have this worthwhile happiness— so long as they want to be in that situation, doing those actions, and do not want in any way to be anywhere else or doing anything else. That is, the only people who will be happy in heaven will be people with a certain character.

The Christian doctrine—Catholic and Protestant—is that heaven is not a reward for good action (for, as we have seen, even on the Catholic view a man can go there without having done any); rather, it is a home for good people. This view receives abundant biblical support in the parable of the laborers in the vineyard (Matthew 20:1-16). Entry to the kingdom of heaven is compared to a situation where the same reward is given to those who have worked the whole day and to those who have worked only one hour. What determines whether they get their reward is their status as workers, that they are developing the vineyard (having accepted the challenge to work when it came), not how many hours work they have done.

The character needed for the inhabitants of heaven is that of perfect goodness. To have a worthwhile happiness in the situation and occupations of heaven a man needs to want to be there doing those things and also to hold true beliefs that that situation and those actions are of supreme value. He must, that is, both desire the good and also have a true belief about where it is to be found.

III

This point enables us to answer the question about why true religious belief matters for getting to heaven. People who come to have different beliefs about whether there is a God, what he is like, and what he has done, will, if they are pursuing the good, do different actions. If they come to believe that there is a God, they will worship God and will seek to make others worshipping people; if they come not to believe, they will not do these things. Someone with a theistic creed different from the Christian one will have a different view about the kind of reverence to be paid to God. If you think that God walked on earth, you are likely to have a different kind of reverence for him than if you think of him merely as a philosopher's first principle, and also a different kind of reverence for men, of whom God became one. A man with a different creed will meditate on different things and practice different kinds of human relationship (e.g., Islam commends a different pattern of family life from that of Christianity.) Thereby, even if both are basically seeking the good, the character of a non-Christian will be different from that of a Christian. If the Christian creed is the true one and so the Christian way to behave the right one, the non-Christian would have to acquire true beliefs and practice different actions before he could enjoy the worthwhile happiness of the Christian heaven. (And, of course, if the Islamic creed is the true one, the reverse change would be required.)

So you need true beliefs simply in order to know which actions are most worth doing — which is necessary before you start doing those actions, and so start on the road to doing them naturally and spontaneously (and so desiring to do them). And you need true beliefs about your situation (e.g., of being redeemed, etc.) if you are to be truly blessed, for then you know wherein to rejoice.

So it is important that we acquire true beliefs, and so we ought to set about so doing. A man who seeks the good will seek to discover what is most worthwhile. Such an honest inquirer may discover the answer on earth. But he may not. Yet since such a person is seeking the good, he has embarked on the way to heaven and would enjoy heaven when he is given information on how to do so. As he will need to make no further choice, God may well give him the information when this earthly life is over. But a man not seeking true beliefs about what is worth doing is not a man of good will.

Once a seeker of the good has been given a true belief about what is good, clearly he will pursue it. But there is and must be a certain stickiness about character, for character is a matter of what you do naturally. If someone has made himself the sort of person who does something naturally, to do anything else is going to be unnatural—to start with. A change will need time and energy.[16]

An extreme example of a man of good will who had made himself thoroughly unfitted for the Christian heaven would be a conscientious Buddhist. If Buddhism really involves the killing of all desire,[17] then clearly the Buddhist is not going to fit into the Christian heaven. For he will not be happy in the activities of knowledge acquisition, worship, and service which are the occupations of the inhabitants of heaven. For happiness involves being glad that you are doing what you are doing, i.e., doing what you want to be doing; and the Buddhist does not want to be doing anything. For a man to come to see that it was good that he should get himself to want things, and then to get himself to want them, might be very hard.

So the answer to my original question is that right religious belief matters because only with it will a man know how he should live, and only if he does live in the right way can he attain the happiness of heaven. For heaven is the community of those who live in the right way and get happiness out of it because they want to live in the right way. By pursuit of the good they have so molded themselves that they desire to do the good. So the answer why God would send the men of natural good will and true belief to heaven is that they are fitted for it. They would enjoy there a supremely worthwhile happiness, and God being perfectly good seeks that for them. But what of those who do not seek the good, who choose to do what is morally bad, and not through a false belief that it is really good but because their will is bad? (I assume in my subsequent discussion that the bad do not have false beliefs about what is good. It will appear that it could easily be made more complicated to deal with the possibility of false belief.)

Clearly there is no point in God sending the bad to heaven as they are, for they would not be happy there. The man who wants to be applauded for what he has not done, who wishes to see the good humiliated and to get pleasure out of the company of similarly malevolent persons, would not be happy pursuing the occupations of heaven.

IV

But cannot the bad be made good in order that they may enjoy heaven? The answer to that question depends on an understanding of the nature and desirability of human choice.

Although young children have often not reached this situation, and (as we shall see later) the old may sometimes have passed beyond this situation, there is a stage in a normal man's life at which he reaches what I may call the normal situation of choice. In this situation he has moral perceptions — he sees some actions as morally good (and some of those as obligatory), other actions as morally bad (and some of those as obligatory not to do). By the morally good action I mean the one which overall is better than alternative actions good to some degree which a man could do instead. Of course a man's judgments may not always be the right ones — he may fail to see of some morally worthwhile acts that they are morally worthwhile. But nevertheless he does have moral perceptions. If a man really believes that some action is a good action (and does not simply think that it is good by normally accepted criteria), he will to some extent desire to do it. He may on balance prefer to be doing something else, but he will in a wide sense desire to some degree to be doing it. For its goodness gives him reason for doing it, and in recognizing its goodness he recognizes that he has such a reason.

A man, however, will also have other desires for lesser goods.

Insofar as a man desires to do some action he will believe that it is in some way a good thing that he do it. For if he desires to do the action, he will desire it because (he believes) there is something good about it. The man who desires to steal a car (rightly) regards it as in some way a good thing that he possess the car. For possession of what gives pleasure is good. The trouble is, of course, that it is more good for other reasons that he refrain from stealing.

A man has to choose between what he sees as overall the best action to do and what he regards as lesser goods. In this situation, it is often said, the strongest desire wins. But if one calls a desire strongest if it is the one on which the man eventually acts, that is a very uninformative tautology; and on any other criterion of "strongest desire" it is often false. A natural way of measuring strength of desires is that a desire is strong insofar as it needs much effort to act against it. Sexual desires are often strong, whether or not men often act on them, because men have to struggle hard not to act on them. In this latter sense of strength of desire the man's situation is indeed one in which there are desires of different strengths to do actions, and also one where he sees the actions as having different degrees of worth. The ordering by strength and the ordering by perceived worth may not be the same. The man has to choose whether to resist strong desires in order to do the morally good action, or to yield to them.

Now people come into existence with a limited range of choice — a limited set of good and evil actions which are for them live possibilities. By our choices (encouraged or frustrated by our bodily condition, mental state, environment, upbringing, friends and enemies)[18] we shift the range of possible choice. By good choices this time there come within our range possibilities for greater good next time, and some evil choices are no longer a possibility. Conversely, by bad choices this time there come within our range possibilities for greater evil next time, and some good choices are no longer a possibility. Further, many of men's strongest desires are for lesser goods, i.e., for the bad. (This is part of what is involved in original sin.) Without effort man will slide toward the bad.

So someone who chooses the good may not do the good action naturally; he may have struggled against his strongest desire in order to do it. But we are so made that what we have to strug-

gle to do to start with will tend eventually to become natural.
That is, the desire to do it will become the strongest desire (as
measured by the strength of resisting it). Among our good actions will be taking measures to control our passions. These are
not under our immediate control — what we are pleased at is
something we cannot immediately help. But we can through a
process of reflecting on what seems to us good often get ourselves to be pleased at its occurrence. The determined pursuit
of the good tends to make a man a man who naturally seeks the
good. Someone will be a good man if he has also a right view
of what the good consists in. If he does he will do naturally, not
merely the actions which he believes good, but actions which
are good, and so he will be fitted for heaven.[19]

However, a man may yield to bad desires against his better
judgment. Now those who (by yielding to such a bad desire) resist a good desire will have such good desires again. But if they
systematically resist desires of a certain kind, they will gradual-
ly become the kind of person to whom such desires do not occur
with any force. Those who refuse to give to charity once may
have a fit of conscience and give more next time. But those who
systematically refuse to give come no longer to regard it serious-
ly as a good thing to give. Giving passes out of the range of their
possible choice. A man who never resists his desires, trying to
do the action which he perceives overall to be the best, grad-
ually allows what he does to be determined entirely by the
strength of his desires (as measured by the difficulty of resisting
them). That is, he eliminates himself (as an agent doing the action of greatest perceived worth or allowing himself to be overcome by strong desire to do an action of lesser worth, or simply
choosing between actions of equal perceived worth). There is
no longer a "he"; having immunized himself against the nag-
ging of conscience, the agent has turned into a mere theatre of
conflicting desires of which the strongest automatically dictates
"his" action.

Now far be it from me to say that that has happened to any
man whom I have ever met; there is a lot more latent capacity
for good in most people than appears on the surface. Nevertheless it is a possibility that a man will let himself be so mastered
by his desires that he will lose all ability to resist them. It is the
extreme case of what we have all too often seen: people increas-
ingly mastered by desires, so that they lose some of their ability

to resist them. The less we impose our order on our desires, the more they impose their order on us.

We may describe a man in this situation of having lost his capacity to overrule his desires as having "lost his soul." Such a man is a prisoner of bad desires. He can no longer choose to resist them by doing the action which he judges to be overall the best thing to do. He has no natural desires to do the actions of heaven, and he cannot choose to do them because he sees them to be of supreme worth. There is no "he" left to make that choice. Perhaps God could make the choice for him, give him a strong desire to do the good, and annihilate all other desires in him. But that would be imposing on an agent something which, while he was still capable of choosing between actions in virtue of their worth, he had in effect chosen not to do — by yielding so continually to temptation. Free will is a good thing, and for God to override it for whatever cause is to all appearances a bad thing.

It might be urged that no man would ever be allowed by God to reach such a state of depravity that he was no longer capable of choosing to do an action because of its overall worth. But in that case God would have prevented people from opting for a certain alternative; however hard a man tried to damn himself, God would stop him. It is good that God should not let a man damn himself without much urging and giving him many opportunities to change his mind, but it is bad that someone should not in the all-important matter of the destiny of his soul be allowed finally to destroy it. Otherwise the situation would be like that of a society which always successfully prevented people who would otherwise live forever from committing suicide. A society certainly has no right to do that, and plausibly even God has no analogous right to prevent people from destroying their own souls.

It may be said that God should not allow someone to damn himself without showing him clearly what he was doing. But a man who simply ignored considerations of worth and gave in continually to his strongest desire could hardly fail to realize that he was becoming a theatre of conflicting desires. He might not know the depth of the happiness which he was losing, nor that it would be prolonged forever in Heaven. He would however know that he was choosing not to be a worthwhile kind of person.

Strangely, it would not necessarily help someone attain the happiness of heaven if God did make it crystal clear to him that heaven existed and provided happiness for the good. For Christian theology emphasizes that the happiness of heaven is something which begins on earth for the man who pursues the Christian way. This is because the pursuit of that way on earth involves starting to do the tasks of heaven — for a short time with limited tools and understanding, with many obstacles including the desires for other things. The Christian on earth has begun to understand the divine nature (by Bible reading, receiving religious instruction, etc.), to worship (in the Eucharist with music, poetry, art, etc.), and to show the divine love to others. But his tools are poor — his mind and his instructors provide weak understanding of the divine nature; his organs and choirs are poor things; and he has many desires to do other things, which need to be eradicated before the Christian way can be enjoyed. Now, given all that, if a man did not seek such a life on earth, why should he seek it if he comes to learn that it can go on forever and provide deep happiness? Either because he wants to live forever or because he wants the happiness. But while someone is seeking to live the good life for those reasons, he will not find the happiness of heaven. For the happiness of heaven is not simply happiness. It is, as we have seen, a special kind of happiness. It is a happiness which comes from doing actions which you know to be supremely good because you want to be doing those supremely good actions. A man who sought the happiness of heaven for *its* own sake could not find it while that was his goal, for it is the happiness which comes from doing certain actions for *their* own sake. The happiness of heaven is a happiness which comes to those who are not seeking it.[20]

True, the news of heaven might provide an initial incentive for a bad man to pursue the good way, which he might later come to pursue for better reasons. (Heaven and hell have often been preached for this purpose.) But clearly, if you encourage a man to pursue happiness (or everlasting life), he is likely to continue to do so. In this way, by pursuing happiness (or everlasting life) rather than goodness, he might fail to find the happiness which he might otherwise have got.[21]

There are good reasons other than to provide an incentive for the bad why God should tell men about heaven. The news of heaven would, for example, show people that God was good and so provide further reason for giving particular content to the good life — that is, for worshipping God. It would also provide encouragement for those who sought to live the good life anyway to know that they could go on doing so forever under circumstances where the obstacles to living that life had been removed.

Perhaps the best compromise would be for God to let people know that there is *some chance* of their going to heaven if they lead a good life [and of "losing their soul" in some sense if they lead a bad life], but only some chance — to avoid to some extent the danger of men pursuing heaven for the wrong reasons and so losing it. And indeed the knowledge situation of most people in most societies has been just this. True, in our secular society someone might not know even that. Yet, as we have already seen, that is not necessarily a bad thing; and also there is the most important point that if one insists that agents had to know that there were such chances before they could be deprived of heaven, this would have the consequence that God would have to promulgate the Gospel independently of the activities of men. If men, in a particular church, are to make known the possibility of heaven, there must be those who otherwise would live in total ignorance of that possibility. It is good that the fate of men should depend in small part on the activity of other men — that men should carry the enormous responsibility of the care of the souls of others.[22]

I conclude that a good God might well allow a man to put himself beyond the possibility of salvation, even without revealing to him the depth of eternal happiness which he was losing. The doctrine of the majority of Christian theologians down the centuries is not, however, merely this, but that such persons suffer eternal physical pain in hell as a punishment for their sins. Now certainly such persons may deserve much punishment. For God gave them life and the opportunity of salvation, but they ignored their creator, hurt his creatures, damaged his creation, and spent their lives seeking trivial pleasures for themselves. But for God to subject them to literally *endless* physical pain (*poena sensus* in medieval terminology) does seem to me to be incompatible with the goodness of God. It seems to have the character of a barbarous vengeance; whatever the evil, a finite number of years of evildoing does not deserve an infinite number of years of physical pain as punishment. The all-important punishment is to be deprived of eternal happiness (this is the *poena damni* in medieval terminology) — a fact which Augustine, a firm proponent of the doctrine of endless physical pain, himself pointed out.[23] This deprivation, I have suggested, is plausibly an inevitable fate of those who have finally rejected the good.[24] It seems to me that the central point of New Testament teaching is that an eternal fate is sealed, at any rate for many, at death, a good fate for the good and a bad fate for the bad. This appears to be the main point of such parables as the sheep and the goats.[25] It is always dangerous to take literally too many minor details of parables (such as the punishment being *αἰώνιος*, about which theologians dispute whether it is properly translated "everlasting"). Given the main point, there seem to be various possible fates for those who have finally rejected the good. They might cease to exist after death. They might cease to exist after suffering some limited physical pain as part of the punishment of their wickedness. Or they might continue to exist forever pursuing trivial pursuits (as amusingly depicted in Bernard Shaw's *Man and Superman*), perhaps not even realizing that the pursuits were trivial. However, the crucial point is that it is compatible with the goodness of God that he should allow a man to put himself beyond possibility of salvation, because it is indeed compatible with the goodness of God that he should allow a man to choose the sort of person he will be.

NOTES

1. *Summa theologiae*, 2a, 2ae, 1.2.
2. For quotations to substantiate this see *Faith and Reason*, ch. 4.
3. *Summa theologiae*, 1a, 2ae, 19.5.
4. *Lumen gentium*, 16.
5. See the saying of Jesus in Luke 12:48 that the servant who did not know his master's will and did things worthy of a beating "shall be beaten with few stripes," in contrast with the servant who knew the master's will and still did not do it who "shall be beaten with many stripes." The point of the saying must lie in the contrast, not in the fact that the ignorant servant would have a small beating. The teaching

of the parable of the talents (e.g., Matthew 25:14-30) seems also to be that what is required of man is to make what he can from what has been given to him, and it is natural to interpret it so as to include in what has been given to a man his religious knowledge.

6. See, e.g., John Hick, *Death and Eternal Life* (London: Collins, 1976).

7. "By a single, uninterrupted and continuous act our minds will be united with God" (*Summa theologiae*, 1a, 2ae, 3.2, ad 4).

8. On the importance of such worship see Richard Swinburne, *The Coherence of Theism* (Oxford: Clarendon Press, 1977), ch. 15.

9. Aquinas claims that in the blessedness of Heaven "the society of friends adds a well-being to blessedness" (*Summa theologiae*, 1a, 2ae, 4.8).

10. And see also Christ's words to his disciples: "Ye which have followed me, in the regeneration when the Son of man shall sit on the throne of his glory, ye also shall sit upon twelve thrones, judging the twelve tribes of Israel" (Matthew 19:28). "Judging" may mean here "ruling over."

11. Bernard Williams affirms the necessary undesirability of eternal life in "The Makropoulos Case" (in his *Problems of the Self* [Cambridge: Cambridge University Press, 1973], ch. 6). But those whom he pictures as necessarily bored in eternity seem to me persons of limited idealism.

12. *Summa theologiae*, 1a, 2ae, 4.1.

13. *Confessions*, 10.23.

14. *Summa theologiae*, 1a, 2ae, 4.5.

15. See *Summa theologiae*, 1a, 2ae, 1-5. Aquinas argues that full *beatitudo* consists in the "activity" (3.2) of "laying hold of our ultimate end," which is, he claims, God, the supreme Good. He has arguments to show that it does not consist in riches, honor, fame, power, bodily well-being, and such. It is necessary for *beatitudo* that one should seek to get the right thing—God—although the attainment of that thing depends on God himself giving it to us. Aquinas holds (1.7) that all men desire *beatitudo*, but some men have false ideas about where it is to be found.

16. Aquinas writes that no one can attain to the vision of God "except by being a learner with God as his teacher" and that "a person becomes a sharer in this learning not all at once but step-by-step in keeping with human nature" (*Summa theologiae*, 2a, 2ae, 2.3; Blackfriars edition [London, 1974], vol. 31, trans. T.C. O'Brien).

17. And I may have misunderstood it here.

18. Christianity has usually insisted on the doctrine that no man can attain salvation without the help of God's grace. Clearly a man needs the help of his fellow Christians both to know about the Chris-

tian way and to begin to follow it, and the help of the church in order to continue to follow it (since following it involves practicing it within the church). Christianity can therefore give content to this doctrine by holding that other Christians and the church are the channels of grace.

19. I have written that "determined pursuit of the good *tends* to make a man a man who naturally seeks the good." And often such determined pursuit achieves its goal with respect to an aspect of a man's life or the whole of that life. Determined pursuit of the good makes people naturally good. Yet such determined pursuit does not always achieve its goal in this life. Some men are so beset by certain tempting desires that, however hard they try, they cannot eradicate them in this life. However, by their efforts such men will have made those desires "extrinsic" to themselves, unwelcome forces impinging from without, no part of their adopted character. God could easily in an afterlife remove such desires without changing the formed characters of men of good will, and he would be expected to allow men's choice to reject such desires finally to have the effect that the desires no longer impinge on men's consciousness.

20. See Christ's saying: "He that findeth his life shall lose it; and he that loseth his life for my sake shall find it" (Matthew 10:39).

21. Recall the concluding verses of Christ's parable of Dives and Lazarus. Dives, in hell, asks Abraham to send Lazarus to warn his five brothers to change their life-style lest they go to hell. He says to Abraham, "If someone goes to them from the dead, they will repent." But Abraham replies: "If they hear not Moses and the Prophets, neither will they be persuaded if one rise from the dead" (Luke 16:29f).

22. On this see Richard Swinburne, *The Existence of God* (Oxford: Clarendon Press, 1979), pp. 187-96.

23. St. Augustine, *Enchiridion*, ch. 102.

24. John 3:19 suggests that sin by itself is its own punishment.

25. Matthew 25:31-46. There are some sayings of Christ's which carry a suggestion that any punishment will be limited. For example, there is the warning to men to be reconciled quickly with their adversaries lest they be thrown into prison: "You shall by no means come out from there until you have paid the last penny" (Matthew 5:26). As John Hick comments (*Death and Eternal Life*, p. 244), "Since only a finite number of pennies can have a last one we seem to be in the realm of graded debts and payments rather than of absolute guilt and infinite penalty."

Divine Conservation, Continuous Creation, and Human Action

PHILIP L. QUINN

Theistic religions make much of the power of God. He is said to be omnipotent or at least almighty. However difficult it may be to give a correct philosophical account of such talk, its religious importance is clear. If God is to merit our worship and trust, he must be powerful enough to make all things serve his good purposes. As A. C. Ewing says, "the doctrine of the omnipotence of God is of great religious importance because in its usual context this alone will give us a guarantee that His good will prevails."[1] But it is not merely that God is powerful enough to shape and control the cosmos of contingent things; all these things depend upon God for their very existence. God, it is said, created the heavens and the earth.

Philosophical theories about the manner in which contingent things depend upon God differ. A minimal theory is that of the deists. According to this view God brought into existence all those things which have begun to exist by creating them. Once having been created, such things continue to exist on their own, without further support from God. God is the divine artificer; he has no need to interfere in the workings of his artifacts after contriving them. Much of theistic tradition, however, goes well beyond this minimal theory to hold that contingent things are continuously dependent upon God for their existence. On this view God not only creates the cosmos of contingent things but also conserves it in existence at every instant when it exists. Weighty philosophical opinion stands behind the doctrine of divine conservation. It is endorsed by Aquinas, Maimonides, and Descartes among our philosophical ancestors, and by Mavrodes and Ross among our philosophical contemporaries.[2]

How does God conserve the contingent denizens of the cosmos? According to many philosophers, divine conservation is nothing but a kind of continuous creation. We have it on good authority that the Mutakallims held:

> The substance, like its indwelling accidents, perishes forthwith upon its creation and is re-created by God so long as He wishes. But every such act of re-creation implies a fresh start in the life-history of substance, so that duration is no more and no less than a process of successive phases of being (hūduth).[3]

Descartes tells us:

> It is as a matter of fact perfectly clear and evident to all those who consider with attention the nature of time, that, in order to be conserved in each moment in which it endures, a substance has need of the same power and action as would be necessary to produce and create it anew, supposing it did not yet exist, so that the light of nature shows us clearly that the distinction between creation and conservation is solely a distinction of the reason.[4]

Berkeley writes to Samuel Johnson:

> Those who have all along contended for a material world have yet acknowledged that *natura naturans* (to use the language of the Schoolmen) is God; and that the divine conservation of things is equipollent to, and in fact the same thing with, a continued repeated creation: in a word, that conservation and creation differ only in the *terminus a quo*.[5]

And Leibniz repeats the theme over and over again. In the *Theodicy* he says:

> . . . we must bear in mind that conservation by God consists in the perpetual immediate influence which the dependence of creatures demands. This dependence attaches not only to the substance but also to the action, and one can perhaps not explain it better than by saying, with theologians and philosophers in general, that it is a continued creation.[6]

In the *New Essays Concerning Human Understanding* he claims:

Thus it is true in a certain sense, as I have explained, that not only our ideas, but also our sensations, spring from within our own soul, and that the soul is more independent than is thought, although it is always true that nothing takes place in it which is not determined, and nothing is found in creatures that God does not continuously create.[7]

And in the correspondence with Clarke he insists:

The soul knows things, because God has put into it a principle representative of things without. But God knows things, because he produces them continually.[8]

It would be easy, though tedious, to multiply quotations. There is more philosophical profit to be derived from trying to explicate the claim that divine conservation is a kind of continuous creation.

In this essay I propose to explore some relations among the concepts of creation, conservation, and continuous creation. First, I shall lay out one theory of their relations that has some intuitive plausibility. I shall next argue that this theory has the unfortunate consequence that human action, as we normally understand it, is impossible. Nevertheless, the theory is of some interest because it has among its consequences some of the things Jonathan Edwards had to say about the relations of God to his creatures. Then I shall present a second theory which, though less attractive, intuitively speaking, than the first, avoids these unwelcome consequences. Finally, I shall argue that the second theory can be interpreted in a way that gives sense to many of the philosophical claims I have quoted above and can be defended against certain objections.

Theoretical Preliminaries

I shall assume throughout that time has the structure of a linear continuum whose ultimate or atomic constituents are durationless instants. I shall use the letter "t," primed as needed, as a variable ranging over instants of time. The letter "x," primed as needed, will serve as a variable ranging over individual things, and the letter "A," primed as needed, will serve as a variable ranging over particular human actions (as opposed to action-types).

I shall make use of six undefined, schematic locutions. The first is "x is contingent." This is to be understood as roughly synonymous with "x is such that possibly it exists and possibly it does not exist." The second is "x exists at t." This is to express the notion of an individual existing at an instant of time. I have elsewhere argued that existence throughout an interval of time can be adequately defined in terms of this notion.[9] I use this locution in such a way that the possibility that an individual exists for only a single instant of time is not precluded. The third is "t is before t'." This is to express the ordinary tenseless relation of temporal priority between temporal instants. It is worth noting that, on the assumption that time is a linear continuum, if one temporal instant is before another, the two are the endpoints of a finite interval that contains a nondenumerable infinity of instants. The fourth is "God at t brings it about that x exists at t." This is to express the idea that God's act at an instant is the sole and total cause of the existence of an individual at that instant. The use of this locution presupposes that God can act at an instant of time. Because God does not have to act by moving some bodily part, I can see no objection to this presupposition.[10] The fifth is "x is performing A at t." This is to capture the concept of a human agent being engaged at an instant in performing some action. Its use does not imply that any human agent can complete any action in a mere instant. The sixth is "x performs A." This is to be understood in such a way that the human agent in question performs the complete action in question.

There are four general definition schemata that will come in handy in my later theory construction. The first two explicate the notion of beginning to exist:

(D1) x begins to exist at t = df x exists at t, and there is no t' such that t' is before t and x exists at t'.

(D2) x begins to exist = df For some t, x begins to exist at t.

If time has a first instant, then, according to (D1), any individual which exists at the first instant begins to exist then and, hence, begins to exist. So if the first instant of time is the instant of the Big Bang, whatever exists at the instant of the Big Bang begins to exist at that instant.[11] Notice too that according to these definition schemata everything which begins to exist will have a first instant of its existence; they rule out the possibility that something begins to exist without having a first instant of its existence. I have elsewhere argued that this possibility should not be precluded by definitional fiat, but I here ignore the complications that would be needed to avoid precluding it as irrelevant to my present purposes.[12] The next two definitions spell out the notion of temporal persistence:

(D3) x persists from t to t' = df t is before t', x exists at t, x exists at t', and, for all t'' such that t is before t'' and t'' is before t', x exists at t''.

(D4) x is a persistent thing = df For some t and t', x persists from t to t'.

According to these definitions a persistent thing is an individual which exists at every instant in some finite closed temporal interval. These definitions obviously do not imply or entail that an individual which persists from one instant to another either begins to exist at the first of these instants or ceases to exist at the second.

With these preliminary points firmly in mind, we can now turn our attention to the task of constructing our first theory of creation, conservation, and continuous creation.

A Theory of Creation and Conservation

Our first theory begins from the attractive intuition that to create an individual is to bring into existence an individual that has never before existed. This intuition is encapsulated in the following two definition schemata:

(D5) At t God creates x = df God at t brings it about that x exists at t, and there is no t' such that t' is before t and x exists at t'.

(D6) God creates x = df For some t, at t God creates x.

These definition schemata properly leave open the question of whether a thing once created persists. They are consistent with the deistic view that at least some created things persist on their own without further divine intervention unless destroyed by God, but they are also consistent with the theistic view that all created things would perish forthwith unless sustained with divine activity since they do not entail that any created thing exists for more than an instant. They also leave open the question of whether created things can exist intermittently after their creation. Hence, they do not preclude the possibility that some creatures exist throughout some temporal interval, then fail to exist throughout a subsequent interval, and finally exist again throughout a still later interval. In short, they do not preclude the possibility that the doctrine of the General Resurrection is true.

The doctrine of creation associated with these definition schemata may be stated as follows:

(P1) For all x, if x is contingent and x begins to exist, then God creates x.

In other words, this doctrine postulates that all contingent things that begin to exist are created by God. If time has a first instant and some contingent things exist at that instant, then by (D1) they begin to exist at that instant, and, hence, by (P1), (D5), and (D6) God creates them at that instant. Contingent things which begin to exist at instants other than the first are created by God at the instants when they begin to exist. But if time has no first instant and there are contingent things which exist always and never begin to exist, those things are never created by God, since there is no time before which those things do not exist. Thus, this doctrine of creation allows the possibility that there are contingent things which are uncreated.

Even so, it may be objected, the doctrine is too strong. Suppose, for example, I cast a bronze statue of Pegasus. My statue, it may be said, is a contingent thing which begins to exist at some instant around the time I finish casting it, yet it is created by me and not by God. The reply is obvious. The fabrication of a statue is not a case of coming to be at all; it is a case of alteration. A certain chunk of stuff alters in respect of some of its properties, shape included. On the other hand, if human persons really begin to exist, then they are created by God. But this is as it should be according to theistic orthodoxy: human persons really come to be, and God creates them.

How are we to incorporate divine conservation into this theory? An appealing intuition is that divine conservation consists of contingent individuals depending for their existence on God's active power at every instant when they exist. This intuition is made more precise by the following two definition schemata:

(D7) At t God conserves x = df x exists at t if and only if God at t brings it about that x exists at t.

(D8) God conserves x = df For all t, at t God conserves x.

According to these definition schemata God's activity is both necessary and sufficient for the existence of those things he conserves at every instant when they exist. They do not imply or entail that there are any persistent things, for they are consistent with the assertion that God never brings about the existence of an individual for more than an instant. But if there are any persistent things whose existence God brings about, those things depend upon God's activity for their existence at every instant when they exist. And, finally, they too leave open the possibility that there are things which exist intermittently.

The doctrine of divine conservation that goes with these definitions may be expressed by means of this postulate:

(P2) For all x, if x is contingent, then God conserves x.

This doctrine is inconsistent with the deistic view that contingent things, once created by God, persist without God's support. Any contingent thing which persists will be such that God brings about its existence at every instant, and throughout every interval, when it exists. And if there are any persistent contingent things which never began to exist and so are, according to this theory of creation, uncreated, they are nonetheless conserved in existence by God whenever they do exist and are, thereby, always dependent upon his activity for their existence. Thus, this doctrine of divine conservation appears to reflect accurately the theistic tenet that every contingent individual depends upon the power of God, and on that power alone, for its existence at every instant when it exists.

Within the framework of the doctrine so far developed, how are we to make sense of the notion of continuous divine creation? If continuous divine creation is to be a kind of creation at all, the most natural way to explicate the notion would appear to be this:

(D9) God continuously creates x = df For all t, x exists at t if and only if at t God creates x.

This definition schema seems natural because it tells us that a continuously created individual is one which exists at an instant just in case at that instant God creates it. Moreover, it allows us to give a sensible interpretation of the Cartesian view that the difference between divine conservation and continuous creation is only a distinction of the reason and of Berkeley's view that they differ only in the *terminus a quo*. According to (D7) a conserved individual is one which exists at an instant just in case God at that instant brings it about that it exists at that instant. But according to (D9) and (D5) a continuously created individual is one which exists at an instant just in case God at that instant brings it about that it exists at that instant and it has not previously existed. Hence, Descartes is right when he says conservation requires the same power and action as creation anew. The only difference between conservation and continuous creation has nothing to do with God's activity or a contingent individual's dependence upon it; it is merely that a continuously created individual, being created, has not previously existed. We think of a created individual as being produced by God after not previously having existed, and we think of a conserved individual as being produced by God even if it has previously existed. The difference lies, not in the divine power at work at the instant when God acts, but in how we conceive of the temporal antecedents of the individual whose existence God's activity then produces.

Thus it would seem that we might complete our doctrine with this additional postulate:

(P3) For all x, if x is contingent and x begins to exist, then God continuously creates x.

Unfortunately, if we take this route, there is a high price to be paid. For suppose, as it seems we have every right to do, that there are some individuals which are contingent and begin to exist. It at least appears to be the case that human persons are such individuals. By (P3) such individuals are continuously created by God, and so by (D9) they exist at any instant just in case God creates them at that instant. But, then, by (D1) they exist at any instant just in case they exist at no prior instant, and hence by (D3) they exist at any instant just in case they have not persisted from any prior instant. Thus, any instant at which they exist must be the first instant at which they exist, and they cannot be persistent things. In short, according to the theory we have constructed, contingent things which begin to exist cannot persist; they can only exist for a single instant. Only contingent things that never begin to exist, if there are any, will be persistent things, provided God conserves them throughout some interval. And so if we ourselves are contingent things that begin to exist, as we usually suppose ourselves to be, then we cannot be persistent things, contrary to our normal common-sense assumptions.

The Edwardian Theory and the Impossibility of Action

Many philosophers would view this consequence of our first theory as a serious embarrassment, perhaps sufficient by itself to show that the theory is untenable. But at least one important philosopher would welcome it. He is Jonathan Edwards, a philosopher who wished to deny that human persons are persistent things. Edwards begins from an assumption about divine conservation which very much resembles the one built into our theory. He says:

> God's upholding created substance, or causing its existence in each successive moment, is altogether equivalent to an *immediate production out of nothing*, at each moment, because its existence at this moment is not merely in part from God, but wholly from him; and not in any part, or degree, from its antecedent existence.[13]

God's upholding contingent things or bringing about their existence at each instant when they exist is, Edwards tells us, equivalent to producing them from nothing at each such instant, because God is their sole and total cause at each such instant. In our theory, (D5), (D7), and (D9) seem to express this thought well enough. But then Edwards goes on to claim:

> If the existence of created substance, in each successive moment, be wholly the effect of God's immediate power, in that moment, with-

out any dependence on prior existence, as much as the first creation out of nothing, then what exists at this moment, by this power, is a *new effect*; and simply and absolutely considered, not the same with any past existence, though it be like it, and follows it according to a certain established method. And there is no identity or oneness in the case, but what depends on the *arbitrary* constitution of the Creator; who by his wise sovereign establishment so unites these successive new effects, that he *treats them as one*, by communicating to them like properties, relations, and circumstances; and so, leads us to regard and treat them as one.[14]

So, for Edwards, contingent things which begin to exist by being created by God out of nothing cannot literally persist through time. They exist only instantaneously. At each instant God creates again anew and weaves for us the illusion of persistence by endowing his new creations with properties and relations similar to those possessed by the old. It is, perhaps, a point of interest about our first theory that it has among its consequences something which so closely approximates this Edwardian doctrine, for it may explain something about the reasoning that led Edwards to these odd views.

Can the theist bite the bullet here and accept the theory, Edwardian consequences and all? I think this can be done only if the theist is prepared to accept some other views that are quite outrageous. One of them concerns human action.

Human actions in the full-blooded sense, because they involve bodily motion, take time to perform. A body can be in motion at an instant of time and have instantaneous velocity and acceleration, but it takes a finite interval of time for a body to move or to make a motion. I had said earlier that I was presupposing that God can act at an instant of time, but I considered myself entitled to this assumption only because God is a pure spirit and does not have to act through a body, so to speak. Perhaps the disembodied spirits of humans could act at an instant too. However, embodied humans can only perform actions in the spatiotemporal world by making motions which span finite temporal intervals. Maybe too there are mental acts that contribute causally to the genesis of human actions but occur at a single instant. Mental willings or decidings, if there are any such things, might be examples of such instantaneous mental acts. Nevertheless, the human actions to which they contribute, such as arm raisings, are not instantaneous. Of course, it makes sense to ask what action, if any, a human agent is performing at an instant of time; at a given instant I may, for instance, be raising my arm. But I do not perform the action of raising my arm, or any other, instantaneously.

Depending on how we individuate human actions, we will find that there are some human actions, or descriptions of human actions, such that the agent need not persist throughout the temporal interval when they, or the events picked out by their descriptions, occur. Thus, for example, a greedy nephew could murder his wealthy aunt by pouring poison in her tea, yet he might die of a heart attack, and hence cease to be, before his aunt drinks the poisoned tea and dies. Or a demented soldier could launch a nuclear warhead by pressing a button, yet he might be shot to death by an alert sentinel before the missile leaves the launching pad. However, there are also some human actions such that the agent must persist throughout the interval when they are being performed just because the agent must be performing them at every instant in that interval. I think the wrist-twisting involved in pouring the poison, the finger-jabbing involved in pressing the button, and many of the other actions philosophers have classified as basic are of this kind. Such actions can be the actions of a single human agent only if that agent exists at every instant when they are being performed. We can express this idea more precisely with the aid of two more definition schemata:

(D10) x performs A from t to t' = df t is before t', x is performing A at t, x is performing A at t', and, for all t'' such that t is before t'' and t'' is before t', x is performing A at t''.

(D11) x persists while performing A = df For some t and t', x performs A from t to t' and x persists from t to t'.

I suggest that if any human agent performs any action, then there is some action such that the agent persists while performing it. Hence I think we are entitled to postulate:

(P4) For all x and A, if x performs A, then, for some A', x persists while performing A'.

Given that human agents are embodied and can perform actions only by making motions, then there are human actions only if human agents are persistent things.

So here is another difficulty for our first theory of creation and conservation. Unless human persons never begin to exist, which seems contrary to both common sense and theistic orthodoxy, they cannot be persistent things. And if human persons are not persistent things, then they perform no actions at all. This conclusion is, I submit, a manifest repugnancy.

There is a certain charming irony in the situation. Jonathan Edwards had wished to deny that created substances are persistent things in order to defend the doctrine of original sin. If human persons do not literally persist through time, then there is, literally speaking, no personal identity through time. What goes proxy for persistence is an arbitrary decision to treat diverse instantaneous human persons as one. But then there is nothing in the nature of things to prevent God from arbitrarily deciding to treat me as one with Adam and to hold me accountable for Adam's eating of the forbidden fruit. But of course it is, literally speaking, also a mistake to say that Adam ate the forbidden fruit, for he could have done that only if he had been a persistent thing. Instead God has arbitrarily decided to treat a number of diverse instantaneous persons as one by endowing them with similar properties and relations and to create the illusion that some one person ate the forbidden fruit. But in sober truth no one of these instantaneous persons ate the forbidden fruit, for no one of them existed long enough to do so. Each one of them existed only long enough to perform an instantaneous part of that momentous action. Hence, no one actually ate the forbidden fruit, and the great Christian doctrine of original sin is not defended but dissolved.[15]

We are, I believe, entitled to hold that there are human actions and, hence, persistent human agents to perform them in the absence of proof to the contrary. Neither the authority of Jonathan Edwards nor our first theory of creation and conservation constitutes such proof. We should, therefore, dissent from the Edwardian view and reject our first theory. Must we also give up on the enterprise of making sense of the doctrine that divine conservation is some sort of continuous creation? I think not. Another theory of the relations among creation, conservation, and continuous creation can be formulated. It does not have the unfortunate Edwardian consequence, yet it allows us to make sense of that strand in theistic tradition which equates divine conservation with continuous creation. After a brief detour I shall turn to the formulation and explanation of this theory.

A Brief Historical and Linguistic Detour

What constraints, if any, does ordinary usage impose upon our talk of creation and conservation? Scotus once proposed an answer:

> Properly speaking, then, it is only true to say that a creature is created at the first moment (of its existence) and only after that moment is it conserved, for only then does its being have this order to itself as something that was, as it were, there before. Because of these different conceptual relationships implied by "create" and "conserve", it follows that one does not apply to a thing when the other does.[16]

However, we have already learned that we cannot accept the whole of this doctrine as a constraint on our theoretical construction if we are to build a coherent, literal account of continuous creation. For (D5) expresses quite adequately the idea that an individual can be created at most once, at the first instant it exists if there is one, and (D5) entails that nothing could be repeatedly or continuously created. This suggests we should be prepared to formulate a technical account of creation which is less restrictive than the one endorsed by Scotus. A plausible candidate for such an account is expressed by the following definition schema:

(D12) At t God creates x = df God at t brings it about that x exists at t.

An individual is created by God at an instant just in case God at that instant brings it about that the individual exists then.

Perhaps our deviations from Scotistic orthodoxy can be kept to a minimum. We can capture handily enough the Scotistic idea that an individual conserved at an instant must be one that was, as it were, there before by means of the following definition schema:

(D13) At t God conserves x = df God at t brings it about that x exists at t, and there is a t' such that t' is before t and x exists at t'.

An immediate consequence of these definitions is the following theorem:

(T1) For all x and t, if at t God conserves x, then at t God creates x.

This looks promising, for it tells us that divine conservation at an instant is a kind of creation at that instant. Of course, creation at an instant does not always imply conservation at that instant; at the first instant of its existence a created individual is not, according to (D13), also conserved.

Our next task is to try to construct on these foundations adequate definitions of continuous creation and continuous conservation. The following formulations have an air of plausibility about them:

(D14) God continuously creates x = df x is a persistent thing, and, for all t, if x exists at t, then at t God creates x.

(D15) God continuously conserves x = df x is a persistent thing, and, for all t, if x exists at t and there is a t' such that t' is before t and x exists at t', then at t God conserves x.

An individual continuously created by God is one which persists throughout at least one finite temporal interval and is created by God whenever it exists. And an individual continuously conserved by God is one which persists throughout at least one finite temporal interval and is conserved by God at all instants, except for the first if there is one, when it exists.

An immediate consequence of this pair of definitions is another theorem:

(T2) For all x, if God continuously creates x, then God continuously conserves x.

What (T2) tells us is that continuous creation is a kind of continuous conservation. But, unfortunately, this is not the result we wanted. We had hoped for an account according to which continuous conservation was either a kind of continuous creation or the very same thing as continuous creation. It is easy to see, however, that continuous conservation of an individual does not imply continuous creation of that individual. Consider an individual which exists at all and only the instants of some finite closed interval whose first instant is t_0 and which is such that God brings about its existence at every one of those instants except t_0. Such an individual is a persistent thing, and so it satisfies the first conjunct of both (D14) and (D15). Since at t_0 it exists while there is no earlier instant at which it exists, the second conjunct of (D15) is true for this case in virtue of a false antecedent. For all other instants in the interval the second conjunct of (D15) is true in virtue of a true antecedent and a true consequent, and for all instants outside the interval the second conjunct of (D15) is true in virtue of a false antecedent. Hence, this individual satisfies (D15) and is continuously conserved by God. Nevertheless, it does not satisfy (D14). At t_0 it exists yet is not created by God, and so for t_0 the second conjunct of (D14) is false.

The moral I wish to draw from this part of the discussion is simple. Since we are looking for a theory according to which divine conservation and continuous creation are at least equivalent, we will do well to make more than minimal departures from what Scotus takes to be proper speech. Scotus himself might have had some sympathy for such a tactic. The sentence immediately following those quoted above is this:

> Nevertheless, the relationship to the cause of the being always remains the same, and if both words signified just this relationship, then they might be truly predicated of the same thing at once, even as "to be from another that gives being" and "to receive being from another" do signify precisely that relation.[17]

My suggestion is that we henceforth think of the words 'creates' and 'conserves' as technical terms and define locutions involving them in such a way as to signify some invariant relationship between God and creatures of the sort Scotus refers to in this passage. Elegance and economy of theory will thereby result.

An Improved Theory of Creation and Conservation

Our second theory differs from the first both in its conception of creation at an instant and in its conception of conservation at an instant. The underlying intuition is that both conceptions are to express a single relationship between God and creatures; this means that the two conceptions should turn out to be definitionally equivalent. We can achieve this result by holding onto (D12), renumbering it for inclusion in our second theory, and modifying our definition schema for conservation at an instant in the following way:

> (D16) At t God creates x = df God at t brings it about that x exists at t.

> (D17) At t God conserves x = df God at t brings it about that x exists at t.

Because (D16) and (D17) have the same definiens, an immediate consequence of these definitions is this theorem:

> (T3) For all x and t, at t God creates x if and only if at t God conserves x.

For God to create or to conserve an individual at an instant is merely for him at that instant to bring about the existence of the individual at the instant. Unlike (D5), (D16) does not entail or imply that a created individual must begin to exist; (D16) only implies that an individual created by God at a time is one whose existence is brought about by God at that time. Unlike (D13), (D17) does not entail or imply that a conserved individual must exist prior to being conserved; (D17) only implies that an individual conserved by God at a time is one whose existence is brought about by God at that time. Thus (D16) and (D17) do succeed in expressing a single relationship between God and creatures. Both (D16) and (D17) leave open the question of whether any individuals God may create and conserve at an instant persist. They are consistent with the deistic view that such things as God creates and conserves at an instant subsequently persist on their own in the absence of further divine support, but they are also consistent with the theistic view that such things could not endure unless upheld by continuing divine activity, since neither entails that such things exist for more than an instant. These definition schemata also leave open the question of whether individuals God creates and conserves at an instant can exist intermittently, and so they do not preclude the possibility of the doctrine of the General Resurrection being true.

Having pre-empted the words 'creates' and 'conserves' for use in (D16) and (D17), we must find other vocabulary to express the ideas of (D5) and (D13). The following definitions accomplish this task:

> (D18) At t God introduces x into existence $=$ df At t God creates x, and there is no t' such that t' is before t and x exists at t'.

> (D19) At t God preserves x $=$ df At t God conserves x, and there is a t' such that t' is before t and x exists at t'.

For the reasons Scotus gives in his first passage cited above, it is probably some conception like that expressed by (D18) that most people have in mind when they think of creation of an individual *ex nihilo*. For the same reasons, it is probably some conception like that expressed by (D19) that most people have in mind when they think of God conserving an individual he has previously created. It should be kept clearly in mind that I claim theoretical utility and not naturalness for my definitions of creation and conservation at an instant.

The doctrine of creation that comes with these definition schemata may be stated as follows:

> (P5) For all x and t, if x is contingent and x exists at t, then at t God creates x.

From (P5) and (T3) it follows that

> (T4) For all x and t, if x is contingent and x exists at t, then at t God conserves x.

In other words, God both creates and conserves contingent things whenever they exist. This is as it should be, since creation at an instant and conservation at an instant are definitionally equivalent. A consequence of (P5), (D1), and (D18) is a doctrine about the special case of creation at an instant which is being introduced into existence by God:

> (T5) For all x and t, if x is contingent and x begins to exist at t, then at t God introduces x into existence.

And a consequence of (P5), (T3), and (D19) is a doctrine about the special case of conservation at an instant which is being preserved at that instant by God:

(T6) For all x and t, if x is contingent, and x exists at t and there is a t' such that t' is before t and x exists at t', then at t God preserves x.

All contingent things which begin to exist are created, conserved, and introduced into existence by God at the instant when they first exist; however, God does not preserve them at that instant. If time has a first instant and some contingent things exist then, they begin to exist then according to (D1), and so God creates, conserves, and introduces them into existence then but does not preserve them then. If time has no first instant and there are contingent things which exist but never begin to exist, then God creates, conserves, and preserves them whenever they exist even though he never introduces them into existence. Hence, (P5) and its consequences are inconsistent with the deistic view that contingent things might exist at a time in the absence of God's creating and conserving activity.

To the objection that agents other than God can introduce into existence contingent things which begin to exist, the reply is as before. Such cases only appear to be cases of beginning to exist; in reality they are cases of alteration. So neither are they cases of introducing something into existence in the strict sense.

In a manner exactly parallel to the way in which we introduced our latest definition schemata for creation and conservation at an instant, we may now formulate definition schemata for continuous creation and continuous conservation. Holding on to (D14), but renumbering it for inclusion in our second theory, we modify (D15) to yield the following results:

(D20) God continuously creates x = df x is a persistent thing, and, for all t, if x exists at t, then at t God creates x.

(D21) God continuously conserves x = df x is a persistent thing, and, for all t, if x exists at t, then at t God conserves x.

According to (D20) individuals God continuously creates persist throughout at least one finite temporal interval and depend for their existence on God's creative activity continuously during that interval and whenever else they may exist. And according to (D21) individuals God continuously conserves persist throughout at least one finite temporal interval and depend for their existence on God's conserving activity continuously during that interval and whenever else they may exist. However, God's creative activity and God's conserving activity are exactly the same. If we substitute in (D20) for the phrase 'at t God creates x' the definiens of (D16) and substitute in (D21) for the phrase 'at t God conserves x' the definiens of (D17), we notice that the resulting schemata have the same definiens. Hence, it is an immediate consequence of the definitions of our second theory that

(T7) For all x, God continuously creates x if and only if God continuously conserves x.

God continuously creates and conserves an individual just in case it is a persistent thing such that it exists at an instant only if God at that instant brings about its existence at that instant. Continuous creation and continuous conservation both consist in total dependence of persistent things upon God's power at every instant of their existence. The difference between them is merely verbal.

The doctrine of continuous divine creation embedded in our second theory is a straightforward consequence of (P5) and (D20). It goes as follows:

(T8) For all x, if x is contingent and x is a persistent thing, then God continuously creates x.

And from (T7) and (T8) it follows that

(T9) For all x, if x is contingent and x is a persistent thing, then God continuously conserves x.

According to (T8) and (T9) any contingent thing that persists will be such that God continuously creates and continuously conserves it, which is to say, brings about its existence at every instant and, hence, throughout every interval when it exists. If there are any persistent contingent things which never begin to exist, they too will be continuously created and conserved by God whenever they exist and will, accordingly, depend upon his activity for their existence when they exist, even though God has not introduced them into existence. Thus, our second theory appears to reflect adequately the theistic view that every contingent thing, even everlasting contingent things if there are any, depends upon God's power, and on his power alone, for its existence at every instant when it exists. Seen in this light, the question of whether the cosmos of contingent things was introduced into existence *ex nihilo* after a period of time when nothing contingent existed becomes relatively unimportant for theistic orthodoxy. But perhaps it is worth emphasizing that our second theory does not entail or imply that any continuously created and conserved individual exists at all times. For this reason it does not preclude the possibility that some persistent and continuously created and conserved things exist intermittently or the possibility that human persons, being such things, are resurrected.

Scotus believed that it is possible, or at least not contradictory to suppose, that something exists for only a single instant. He says:

> I claim that there is no contradiction that some being should have being (*esse*) only for an instant, for the instant itself passes suddenly, so that it exists, so to speak, instantaneously.[18]

If there were such an individual what would our second theory have to say about it? Since such an individual is obviously contingent, (P5) says that God creates it at the single instant when it exists, and (T4) tells us that God also conserves it at that instant. Because it clearly begins to exist at that instant, (T5) tells us that at that instant God introduces it into existence. But according to (D19) God never preserves it, since it never exists before that instant. And because it is not a persistent thing, (D20) and (D21) inform us that God neither continuously creates nor continuously conserves it. So it is an individual which is created and instantaneously conserved at the instant when it is introduced into existence but is neither conserved nor preserved after that instant.

Consider another odd possibility. Suppose there were an individual which existed at all and only those instants which correspond to the integers under some order-preserving mapping of the reals one-one onto the whole infinite temporal continuum. What would our second theory have to say about such a peculiar individual? Because such an individual exists only at a denumerably infinite, discretely ordered number of instants, it is not a persistent thing. Hence, according to (D20) and (D21) it is neither continuously created nor continuously conserved by God. Moreover, since there is no first instant of its existence,

(D18) tells us that it is not introduced into existence by God. However, because it is obviously contingent, (P5) says that at each of the denumerably infinite number of instants when it does exist God creates it, and (T4) adds that God also conserves it at each of those instants. Furthermore, (T6) tells us that God also preserves it at each of those instants. Though it is strange, the example illustrates an important point. In our second theory the definitionally equivalent notions of creation at an instant and conservation at an instant are the fundamental ideas. The concepts of continuous creation and continuous conservation are not only defined in terms of them but also restricted in their application to the rather special case of persistent things. Nevertheless, since many of the contingent individuals we encounter in experience seem to be persistent things, the notions of continuous creation and conservation do have some theoretical utility for theology.

So think for a moment about a commonplace, persistent contingent thing. According to (T8) and (T9) we may say of it that God both continuously creates and continuously conserves it. Thus we may agree with Berkeley that its continued divine conservation *is in fact the same thing* as a continued, repeated creation. According to (P5) and (T4) we may also say of it that at every instant in any interval throughout which it persists God both creates and conserves it at that instant. Hence, we may also agree with Descartes that in order to be conserved at each moment in which it endures, it has need of *the same power and action* as would be necessary to produce and create it anew, supposing it did not yet exist.

It is not hard to see that our second theory does not fall prey to the objection that it has the outrageous Edwardian consequence which justified us in rejecting our first theory. Suppose there are some contingent individuals that begin to exist. According to (T5) and (D18), at the instant when such an individual first exists God creates it and thereby introduces it into existence. This by itself does not guarantee that any such individuals will persist, but let us assume in addition that some of them do persist. Then, by (T8) and (T9) God continuously creates and conserves these individuals. However, all this implies, according to (D16), (D17), (D20), and (D21), is that at every instant when such individuals exist God at that instant creates and conserves them, or brings about their existence at that instant, and that God exercises this creative power throughout at least one finite interval when such creatures persist. Since our present theory allows that God can, so to speak, create an individual over and over again, even though he can only introduce a given individual into existence once, it is consistent with a situation in which God continuously creates a persistent individual he has also introduced into existence. Or, to put it another way, because God can repeatedly create a single individual at every instant in a finite interval throughout which it persists, God can repeatedly create, or recreate, one and the same individual. Hence, contingent things once introduced into existence by God's creative power can also persist, dependent at each subsequent instant when they exist on the continuing creative and conserving activity of the same divine power that introduced them into existence in the first place. So if we are contingent things that begin to exist, as we normally suppose ourselves to be, we can also be persistent things, in accord with our usual assumptions, and yet be introduced into existence by God and sustained so long as we exist by his creative and conserving activity.

I can imagine someone objecting to our second theory simply because it does not rule out this possibility. No one, it might be said, not even an omnipotent being, can create one and the same individual more than once. But why not? Perhaps the objector will appeal to some principle like the following:

> (P6) For all x and x', t and t', if God at t brings it about that x exists at t, God at t' brings it about that x' exists at t', and t is diverse from t', then x is diverse from x'.

But this principle is far from being obvious, self-evident, or otherwise epistemically compelling. Once we have distinguished it from the more plausible principle that God cannot introduce a single individual into existence on more than one occasion — a principle built into our theory by virtue of (D18) — (P6) loses whatever intuitive appeal it may initially have had. In addition, it is worth noting that many orthodox theists would reject (P6) and its ilk on the grounds that they are in conflict with the doctrine of the General Resurrection. Such theists will hold that some human persons at least are such that God at one instant brings it about that they exist at that instant, when he introduces them into existence, and God at another instant brings it about that they exist at that instant, when on the Day of Judgment he resurrects them from the dead after an interval of nonexistence. I have never seen a decisive argument against this view, and so I conclude that the objection is at best inconclusive. Therefore, I also conclude that our second theory does provide a coherent reconstruction of the theological doctrines of creation and conservation and an adequate explication of the way in which a certain sort of divine conservation is, as many theists have claimed, a kind of continuous creation. As far as I can see, it gives us a clarified and precise formulation of a theory endorsed by a distinguished tradition of philosophical theists and so merits serious scrutiny by contemporary philosophers of religion.[19]

NOTES

1. A. C. Ewing, *Non-Linguistic Philosophy* (New York, 1968), p. 252.

2. Thomas Aquinas, *Summa theologiae*, pt. 1, q. 104, 1; Moses Maimonides, *The Guide for the Perplexed*, pt. 1, ch. 69; René Descartes, *Meditations* III; George I. Mavrodes, *Belief in God* (New York, 1970), p. 70; James F. Ross, *Philosophical Theology* (Indianapolis, 1969), p. 254.

3. Majid Fakhry, *Islamic Occasionalism* (London, 1958), p. 42.

4. René Descartes, *Philosophical Works*, vol. 1, ed. E. S. Haldane and G. T. R. Ross (New York, 1955), p. 168.

5. George Berkeley, *Works*, vol. 2, ed. A. A. Luce and T. E. Jessop (London, 1950), p. 280.

6. G. W. Leibniz, *Theodicy*, ed. W. Stark (New Haven, 1952), p. 139.

7. G. W. Leibniz, *New Essays Concerning Human Understanding*, trans. A. G. Langley (New York, 1896), pp. 15-16.

8. G. W. Leibniz, *The Leibniz-Clarke Correspondence*, ed. H. G. Alexander (Manchester, 1956), p. 41.

9. Philip L. Quinn, "Existence throughout an Interval of Time, and Existence at an Instant of Time," *Ratio* 21 (1979): 1-12.

10. Of course I do not mean to suggest that this notion is unproblematic in all respects. To my mind the most difficult question it raises is this: How is it possible for God to bring about the existence of any

concrete substance distinct from himself? Perhaps even an omnipotent being can only bring about changes either in his own states or properties or in the states or properties of things whose existence does not depend upon his activity. If this were so, theism would seem to be in danger of collapsing either into Spinozistic pantheism, on the one hand, or into a Platonic theory according to which God is a mere demiurge, on the other. For discussion of related issues see Robert A. Oakes, "Classical Theism and Pantheism: A Victory for Process Theism?" *Religious Studies* 13 (1977): 167-73, and Philip L. Quinn, "Divine Conservation and Spinozistic Pantheism," *Religious Studies* 15 (1979): 289-302.

11. So if time begins with the Big Bang and God is everlasting rather than timeless, God begins to exist then, too. This sounds unorthodox because we usually think of things which begin to exist as doing so after a prior interval of nonexistence. Needless to say, no such thing is in this case implied about God. Nor is it implied that he is contingent or dependent for his existence upon the activity of some other being.

12. Philip L. Quinn, "Existence throughout an Interval of Time, and Existence at an Instant of Time."

13. Jonathan Edwards, *Works*, vol. 3, ed. C. A. Holbrook (New Haven, 1970) p. 402.

14. Ibid., pp. 402-3.

15. If our various instantaneous Adams were Cartesian persons, that is, unextended minds tied to extended bodies, then perhaps only one of them instantaneously decided to eat the forbidden fruit, even though his body did not last long enough actually to consume the forbidden fruit. But which of our Adams should God then blame and punish for eating the forbidden fruit — the one who decided to eat it or those whose bodies actually consumed it? The former did not eat the fruit, and the latter did not decide to eat it. Or maybe all the Adams whose bodies consumed the fruit had the intention of eating the fruit and were on that account blameworthy. But God did not punish any of them. And how could a just God punish the later Adams who regretted the intentions of their predecessors and whose bodies did not consume the fruit? Perhaps the Edwardian theorist would answer by saying that since, on his view, each of us is made up of instantaneous persons and yet we think it obviously just to punish, for example, later Charles Mansons for the deeds of earlier Mansons, we ought to find it no less just that God punishes later Adams for the disobedience of earlier Adams. I confess I do not find this answer persuasive. It seems to me that if we actually held the Edwardian theory, we should not think it obviously just to punish later Mansons for the deeds of earlier Mansons.

16. John Duns Scotus, *God and Creatures: The Quodlibetal Questions*, trans. F. Alluntis and A. B. Wolter (Princeton, 1975), p. 276.

17. Ibid.

18. Ibid., p. 277.

19. I read preliminary drafts of this paper at Brown University, the University of Rochester, and the Notre Dame Conference on the Existence and Nature of God. William P. Alston, Roderick M. Chisholm, and Ernest Sosa gave me extensive written comments on various drafts; George Mavrodes, Alvin Plantinga, Allen Renear, Richard Taylor, and Edward Wierenga made especially useful remarks in discussion. I am grateful to these people, and others, for their help with formulating my theories on this theological topic.

Maximal Power

THOMAS P. FLINT

AND

ALFRED J. FREDDOSO

Christians profess that God is almighty. He has created the world and conserves it in being. Whatever can or does occur is within his control. His great power guarantees the fulfillment of his providential designs.

Theologians and philosophers have typically commenced their explications of divine power with the assertion that God is omnipotent, i.e., that in some sense or other God can do everything. But Peter Geach has recently charged that this assertion is wrongheaded:

> When people have tried to read into 'God can do everything' a signification not of Pious Intention but of Philosophical Truth, they have only landed themselves in intractable problems and hopeless confusions; no graspable sense has ever been given to this sentence that did not lead to self-contradiction or at least to conclusions manifestly untenable from the Christian point of view.[1]

Geach goes on to argue that in all probability any philosophically adequate analysis of omnipotence will have the consequence that in order to be omnipotent an agent has to be able to act in morally reprehensible ways. For instance, it seems reasonable to think that any omnipotent being must have the power, whether or not it is in fact exercised, to perform actions which constitute the breaking of his previously made promises. Yet Christians have traditionally believed that God is impec-

81

cable, i.e., absolutely incapable of such behavior. Once God has promised to send his Son, for example, it appears that he no longer even has the power not to send him. But this could not be true if God were omnipotent. In short, omnipotence on any plausible construal turns out to be incompatible with impeccability.

Nelson Pike had earlier reached the same conclusion by a somewhat different route.[2] Accepting the common view that an omnipotent being is one who can bring about any consistently describable state of affairs, Pike argues that some consistently describable states of affairs are necessarily such that anyone who brings them about is morally blameworthy for so doing. So any agent capable of bringing about such a state of affairs is also capable of acting in a morally reprehensible way and hence is not impeccable in the sense specified above.

Pike responds to this dilemma by urging us to abandon the belief that the person who is God lacks the ability to act in a morally blameworthy fashion. But Geach testily (though correctly, we believe) dismisses this suggestion as patently unorthodox. He counsels us instead to jettison the belief that God is omnipotent. We must simply be careful to distinguish the suspect proposition that God is omnipotent from the theologically central proposition that God is almighty. The latter entails, for instance, that God has power over all things, that he is the source of all power, and that his intentions cannot be thwarted; but it is compatible with the evident truth that there are many things that an agent with all of God's attributes — including, most notably, impeccability — cannot do.

At first Geach's "way out" seems little more than a verbal ploy. After all, it is hardly self-evident that being almighty differs from being omnipotent, or that having power *over* all things differs from having the power *to do* all things (or, as we prefer to say, having maximal power). Nonetheless, further reflection reveals that Geach's position does not essentially depend on the dubious claim that the terms 'almighty' and 'omnipotent' are normally used to express two distinct concepts. Rather, it depends only on the more plausible claim that there are two distinct concepts to be expressed. And here, we believe, Geach is correct.

The term 'almighty', as he uses it, expresses a properly religious concept, i.e., a concept whose explication is subject to overtly theological constraints. To say that God is almighty is to attribute to God all the power that a being with his nature can have.[3] This way of characterizing God's power is not very informative, since it gives one no more insight into the nature of God or the extent of his power than is had antecedently from the sources of revelation. However, there is no danger that the belief that God is almighty will engender any pernicious theological consequences. Most importantly, we can know a priori that it is possible for an agent to be both almighty and impeccable, since this possibility is already explicitly packed into the notion of being almighty.

The term 'omnipotent', on the other hand, is used by Geach to express what we might call a properly secular concept, i.e., one whose explication is subject only to those nontheological constraints which emerge from a careful consideration of the ordinary notion of power and of the relation of power to other properties. It is clear, for instance, that an analysis of omnipotence should not be constructed so as to ensure that there cannot be a morally imperfect omnipotent agent, or a non-omniscient omnipotent agent, or an agent who is only contingently or perhaps even only temporarily omnipotent. But God cannot be an agent of any of these types. So even if God has all the power that a being with his nature can have, there is no a priori guarantee that he has maximal power, absolutely speaking. If Geach is right, then all our evidence points to just the opposite conclusion, viz., that God does not have, indeed cannot have, maximal power.

We concur with Geach that almightiness and omnipotence are distinct properties. However, we will argue in what follows that an orthodox believer need not for this reason give up the hallowed belief that God is omnipotent. For, *pace* Geach, an adequate analysis of maximal power will show that God can be both almighty and omnipotent; and, *pace* both Geach and Pike, such an analysis will show that it is possible for an agent — even a divine agent — to be both omnipotent and impeccable. We will begin by proposing five conditions of philosophical adequacy for an account of maximal power, indicating in the footnotes which of these conditions are not satisfied by one or another of the numerous recent attempts to explicate omnipotence. Then we will present an analysis which meets all five conditions and argue that it is both philosophically adequate and theologically benign.

I

1. Our first condition of adequacy is that an analysis of maximal power should be stated in terms of an agent's power to actualize or bring about states of affairs. (Since we are assuming that there is an exact isomorphism between states of affairs and propositions, we can also speak equivalently of an agent's power to make propositions true.) Though this condition is now widely accepted, some writers have employed the alternative strategy of casting their accounts of omnipotence in terms of an agent's ability to perform tasks, where a task is expressed linguistically by the nominalization of a verb phrase rather than, like a state of affairs, by the nominalization of a complete declarative sentence. The problems with this alternative strategy are well known. Suppose we claim that an agent S is omnipotent just in case S can perform any logically possible task, i.e., any task which is possibly such that someone performs it. This proposal rules out Smith as omnipotent simply on the ground that Smith cannot perform the logically possible task of saying something which is (at the same time) being said only by Jones. Yet it is clear intuitively that this fact about Smith in no way points to a lack of power on his part. Moreover, when we attempt to amend our analysis by claiming that S is omnipotent just in case S has the power to perform any task that it is logically possible *for* S to perform, we find that we are forced to count as omnipotent the notorious weakling Mr. McEar, who is capable of scratching his left ear but essentially incapable of performing any other task.[4]

Such difficulties are obviated by our first condition. For the state of affairs of Smith's saying something which is being said only by Jones is logically impossible and thus unproblematically not within anyone's power to actualize, whereas the state of affairs of Jones's (or: someone's) saying something which is being said only by Jones may well be one which agents other than Jones can actualize and which we should expect an omnipotent being to have the power to actualize.

Nevertheless, even though our first condition is common-place today, few writers on omnipotence have explicitly entertained the following question: Is it possible for one agent to actualize (and hence to have the power to actualize) a state of affairs consisting in or at least involving in some way the free actions of other agents? If we assume a compatibilist account of freedom, the answer to this question is uncontroversially affirmative. For it is obviously possible for a suitably powerful and aptly situated agent to bring it about that another agent has desires or needs and also opportunities that are together causally sufficient for his behaving freely (in this compatibilist sense) in a specified way. So on this view of freedom, bringing about the free actions of others is not relevantly different from actualizing states of affairs that in no way involve the free actions of others. In both sorts of cases the agent in question simply does something which, in conjunction with other operative causal factors, is sufficient for the obtaining of the state of affairs in question.

However, we believe along with many others that there are good reasons for rejecting this account of freedom in favor of the position that every free action must involve the occurrence of an event for which there is no antecedent sufficient causal condition — an event, that is, which has only an agent and no other event as its cause. Given this libertarian conception of freedom, there is a clear and familiar sense of 'actualize' in which it is logically impossible for one agent to actualize another agent's free actions. Following Alvin Plantinga, we call this sense of actualization *strong actualization*.[5] Roughly, an agent S strongly actualizes a state of affairs p just when S causally determines p's obtaining, i.e., just when S does something which in conjunction with other operative causal factors constitutes a sufficient causal condition for p's obtaining. Since an agent's freely performing (or, perhaps better, freely endeavoring to perform) a given action cannot have a sufficient causal condition, it follows straightforwardly that no such state of affairs can be strongly actualized by anyone other than the agent in question.

But even granted the libertarian conception of freedom, there is a weaker sense of actualization — discussed in rather different contexts by both Plantinga and Roderick Chisholm[6] — in which one agent can actualize (and hence can have the power to actualize) the free actions of another. In such cases the agent in question, by his actions or omissions, strongly brings it about that another agent S is in a situation C, where it is true that if S were in C, then S would freely act in a specified way. For instance, a mother might actualize her child's freely choosing to have Rice Krispies for breakfast by limiting his choices to Rice Krispies and the hated Raisin Bran. Or she might bring it about that the child freely donates his allowance to a relief agency by telling him poignantly of the plight of those who do not have enough to eat. In short, it is a familiar truth that one agent may contribute causally to the free actions of another in any number of ways which stop short of being incompatible with the other's acting freely. In such cases it seems perfectly legitimate to say that the one has actualized the other's acting freely in the way in question. Again adopting Plantinga's terminology, we will call this sense of actualization *weak actualization.* Further, it is not only the free actions of another which a given agent may weakly actualize. In addition, an agent S may weakly actualize a state of affairs p *through the mediation of* the free actions of another agent S^*. This occurs when S weakly actualizes S^*'s freely acting in such a way as to bring about p. Thus, in the second of the above examples, the mother weakly actualizes not only her son's freely donating his allowance to a relief agency but also—among others—the state of affairs of someone's hunger being alleviated.

We want to insist that in an analysis of omnipotence the term 'actualize' (or 'bring about') should be construed broadly to include both strong and weak actualization. For it is intuitively evident that a person's power is normally judged in large measure by his ability to influence the free actions of others in one or another of the ways intimated above, e.g., by restricting their options, or by providing them with information or opportunities, or by commanding them, or by persuading or dissuading them, etc. So an omnipotent being should be expected to have the maximal amount of this sort of power. This underscores nicely the impressive nature of maximal power, extending as it does even to the free actions of others. On the other hand, even though the use of this liberal sense of actualization helps us to capture the pervasiveness of an omnipotent agent's power, it also points to an almost universally ignored limitation on that power. We will discuss this limitation below.[7]

2. Our second condition is that an omnipotent being should be expected to have the power to actualize a state of affairs p only if it is logically possible that someone actualize p, i.e., only if there is a possible world W such that in W someone actualizes p. We take this claim to be self-evident.

One generally acknowledged consequence of this condition of adequacy is that the scope of an omnipotent agent's power is limited to logically contingent states of affairs, where a logically contingent state of affairs is one that possibly obtains and also possibly fails to obtain. However, it should be obvious that an analysis of maximal power will not by itself determine just which states of affairs are logically contingent and which are not. Indeed, one could trivialize the consequence in question by espousing the extreme view, sometimes attributed to Descartes, that every state of affairs is logically contingent. Or one might weaken it considerably by embracing the slightly more modest position — and perhaps this is what Descartes actually had in mind — that many allegedly paradigmatic necessary truths, e.g., logical laws or simple mathematical truths, are in fact logically contingent. We do not endorse such views, but nothing we say about maximal power itself will rule them out. Their truth or falsity must be decided independently.

Also, we will explicitly assume below that all states of affairs (and propositions) are tensed. If this assumption is correct, then it is reasonable to think that at least some logically contingent past-tense states of affairs are not possibly such that someone actualizes them.[8] For instance, one might hold that even though it is logically possible for someone to bring it about that Jones will someday be in Chicago, it is logically impossible that anyone ever bring it about that Jones has already been in Chicago. Again, however, an account of maximal power will not by itself decide whether such a claim is true.[9]

3. Many contemporary philosophers not only have accepted our first two conditions of adequacy but also have taken them to be sufficient by themselves. This is evident from the widespread acceptance, until fairly recently, of analyses equivalent to the following:

> (A) S is omnipotent if and only if for any state of affairs p, if there is a world W such that in W someone actualizes p, then S has the power to actualize p.

However, philosophers at least as far back as Aristotle have re-alized that if the past is in some sense necessary, then there are further, purely temporal, restrictions on the power of any agent. The medievals, in fact, had a moderately well articu-lated theory of temporal (*per accidens*) modality, from which it follows that at any given time there are states of affairs which meet the condition specified in (A) and yet are such that they cannot be within the power of any agent to actualize. Inter-estingly, even those like Aquinas, who held that God is not "in time," recognized this sort of restriction on God's power.

So, for instance, suppose that Jones played basketball two days ago. Then, the claim goes, not only is it *true* now that Jones once played basketball, but it is also *necessary* now that Jones once played basketball. That is, in any possible world just like ours prior to the present moment t, it is true at t and at every moment after t that Jones once played basketball. And from this it follows that no one can *now* have the power to ac-tualize the following state of affairs:

(1)   Its being the case that it will be true at some time that Jones has never played basketball.

For it is a minimal and noncontroversial constraint on any agent's having the power at a time t to actualize a state of af-fairs p that there be a possible world W just like ours prior to t such that at t in W someone actualizes p.[10] But, the argument continues, there is no such world in the case of (1). Neverthe-less, (1) satisfies the condition laid down in (A), since it is easy enough to conceive of a possible world in which someone ac-tualizes it. Such an agent might, for example, prevent Jones's coming into existence or arrange for him not to play basketball for a long time after his birth. So it is logically possible for some one to have the power to actualize (1), even though it is logical-ly impossible that both (a) the world have the history it has had until now and (b) someone now have the power to actualize (1). Furthermore, there are any number of states of affairs which are like (1) in these respects. So any adequate account of omnipotence must be relativized to a time. In addition, these purely temporal restrictions on power may vary not only from moment to moment but also from possible world to possible world. And so an account of omnipotence should also be rela-tivized to a possible world. Hence, our analyzandum should be

"S is omnipotent at t in W," and we should incorporate into our analysis the purely temporal restrictions on any agent's power.

This argument rests on two metaphysical presuppositions. The first is that states of affairs (and propositions) are tensed. We find this claim both natural and defensible, and so we accept it. (However, it may be possible for the friends of "tenseless" propositions to recast the argument in their own idiom.) One important consequence is that some logically contingent states of affairs may obtain at some times and not at others within the same possible world. For instance, the state of affairs of Jones's having played basketball does not obtain before Jones plays basketball for the first time but always obtains afterwards. Again, the state of affairs of its being the case that Jones will play basketball may obtain now, but it will not obtain after Jones plays basketball for the last time. Further, some states of affairs may first obtain, and then not obtain, and still later obtain again. An example is the present-tense state of affairs of Jones's (now) playing basketball.

The second metaphysical presupposition is that it is logically impossible that someone travel into the past. This claim, though eminently reasonable, has been challenged of late by several writers, who have asserted in effect that there are no purely temporal restrictions on any agent's power.[11] These philosophers would say that in the case alluded to above it is at least conceivable that someone now travel backwards two days into the past and find himself in a position to prevent Jones from playing basketball. Assuming that Jones has played basketball just this one time, our time traveler would have it within his power to actualize (1). If such a scenario is coherent, it may not be incompatible with our analysis of maximal power, since our third condition of adequacy is simply that an account of omnipotence should accommodate the (epistemic) possibility that there are purely temporal restrictions on the power of an omnipotent agent. We will satisfy this condition by claiming that an omnipotent agent should be expected to have the power at t in W to actualize p only if there is a world W^* such that (i) W^* shares the same history with W at t and (ii) at t in W^* someone actualizes p. Perhaps a proponent of the conceivability of time travel can find a plausible interpretation of the notion of two worlds sharing the same history that allows him to accept this third condition while maintaining that it adds no restrictions on power beyond those already embodied in our second condition of adequacy. (We will return shortly to the notion of sharing the same history.) On the other hand, it may be that any theory of time travel is incompatible with our suggestion for satisfying the third condition. If this is the case, then so much the worse for time travel.

Two points of clarification should be made here. First, we assume that it is logically possible for agents to actualize future-tense states of affairs. For instance, an agent may bring it about at t that Jones will be in Chicago within two hours or that Jones will be in Chicago two hours after t. (Below we will claim that an agent brings about a future-tense state of affairs by bringing it about that a given present-tense state of affairs will obtain at the appropriate future time. So someone brings it about at t that Jones will be in Chicago within two hours by bringing it about that the present-tense state of affairs of Jones's being in Chicago will obtain within two hours after t.) Some may even go so far as to say that where p is a present-tense state of affairs, it is not possible for any agent S to bring it about at t that p obtains at t. That is, S's actualizing p cannot be simultaneous with p's obtaining but must rather precede p's obtaining. If this is so, then every instance of actualization involves the actualization of a future-tense state of affairs. In any case, it is reasonable to expect that an agent who is omnipotent at t will have extensive control over what can happen at any time after t—subject to the restriction which will be set down by our fourth condition of adequacy discussed below.

Second, it should be noted that our third condition of adequacy does not by itself rule out the possibility that someone have the power to bring about (as opposed to alter) the past. This is a separate issue which, as noted above, falls under our second condition of adequacy. So, for example, if it is logically possible that someone now, given the history of our world, brings it about that Carter was elected president in 1976, then an omnipotent agent now has the power to actualize this past-tense state of affairs. Given that Carter was in fact elected in 1976, the argument presented at the beginning of this section does not by itself rule out such backward causation. Again, this is an issue that must be decided independently.

We claimed above that an omnipotent being should be expected to have the power at t in W to actualize p only if there is a world W^* such that (i) W^* shares the same history with W at t and (ii) at t in W^* someone actualizes p. But so far we have said nothing about what it is for two worlds to share the same history at a given time. Perhaps it is not fair to demand that one who gives an analysis provide an exact characterization of each concept used in that analysis, especially when those concepts are tolerably clear on their own. Nevertheless, in this case we feel obligated to say something more, since the concept in question is open to seemingly acceptable construals which would undermine the adequacy of our account of maximal power.

Consider, for instance, the following "natural" explication of sharing the same history:

(2) W shares the same history with W^* at t if and only if for any state of affairs p and time t^* earlier than t, p obtains at t^* in W if and only if p obtains at t^* in W^*.

Since we are assuming that states of affairs are tensed, if we take (2) together with the analogue of the law of bivalence for states of affairs, the net effect is that W can share the same history with W^* at t only if W also shares the same present and future with W^* at t, i.e., only if W is identical with W^*. For among the states of affairs that obtain at any time prior to t in W are future-tense states of affairs which specify exactly what will be true in W at and after t. Moreover, even if we deny that the law of bivalence holds for so-called "future contingent" states of affairs, so that no such state of affairs ever obtains, (2) will still be unacceptable. For on the most popular construal of the notion of a future contingent, a state of affairs is a future contingent at a given time only if it is future-tense and not causally necessary at that time. So even when we make an exception for future contingents, it still follows from (2) that W and W^* share the same history at t only if they share at t what we might call their causally necessitated futures. Such a result is particularly unwelcome when one is trying to explicate maximal power, since it is generally conceded that an agent who is omnipotent at t has the power at t to bring about events whose occurrence is in some sense contrary to nature.[12]

Our own account of two worlds sharing the same history at a given time, which is Ockhamistic in inspiration, has been set out in detail in another place.[13] So we will simply outline it rather broadly here. The basic insight involved is that what is temporally independent — or, to use Chisholm's phrase, rooted in the present — at any given time can be specified in terms of the present-tense (or, as we prefer to say, immediate) states of affairs which obtain at that time. All nonimmediate, or temporally dependent, states of affairs that obtain at a time t obtain at t only in virtue of the fact that the appropriate immediate states of affairs did or will obtain at moments other than t. So, for instance, the nonimmediate state of affairs of Jones's having played basketball obtains now in virtue of the fact that the immediate state of affairs of Jones's playing basketball obtained at some past time. Likewise, the nonimmediate state of affairs of its being the case that Jones will play basketball obtains now in virtue of the fact that Jones's playing basketball will obtain at some future time. This is why it is reasonable to believe that an agent brings it about that Jones will play basketball only *by* bringing it about that Jones's playing basketball will obtain.

Our claim is that for any moment t in a world W there is a set k of immediate states of affairs which determines what obtains at t in a temporally independent way, i.e., what obtains at t but does not obtain at t in virtue of what occurs at moments other than t. We call k the *submoment* of t in W and say that k obtains in W when and only when each of its members obtains in W. Then W and W^* share the same history at t if and only if they share all and only the same submoments, obtaining in exactly the same order, prior to t. Since no future-tense state of affairs is immediate or, consequently, a member of any submoment, it follows that W and W^* may share the same history at t even if their futures are radically diverse at t — and this diversity may extend even to their laws of nature at and after t or to events contrary to the laws of nature that they share at or after t.

Given this general picture, the most pressing task is to provide a plausible characterization of the distinction between immediate and nonimmediate states of affairs. However, our account of this distinction is much too complicated to be presented in passing here. Since it has been worked out in sufficient detail elsewhere, we will simply note one result which will become relevant below. As far as we can tell, this is the only consequence of what we say about the purely temporal restrictions on power that may prove troublesome for our claim that even a divine being may have maximal power.

According to our explication of immediacy, states of affairs involving present-tense propositional attitudes directed at future-tense propositions, e.g.,

(3) Jones's believing that Smith will arrive at 2:00 P.M.

and (4) Jones's promising that Smith will receive a gift,

are immediate unless they entail the future-tense propositions which they involve.[14] On the other hand, if these entailments do hold, then such states of affairs are nonimmediate and hence not members of any submoment. But now consider the following states of affairs:

(5) God's believing that Smith will be saved

and (6) God's promising that Smith will be saved.

Since (5) and (6) both entail that Smith will be saved, each is on our account nonimmediate and hence not eligible for membership in a submoment. This is a welcome result in the case of (5), since it enables us to reconcile divine foreknowledge with human freedom. In short, even if (5) has already obtained, there may still be a world W such that (i) W shares the same history with our world at the present moment and yet (ii) Smith is never saved in W. So even if it has already been true that God believes that Smith will be saved, Smith may still have it within his power to bring it about that he will never be saved. However, this same result is somewhat more troublesome in the case of (6) — for reasons that we will discuss in some detail at the end of this essay.[15]

4. Some might suspect that what we have already said is sufficient for explicating maximal power. For at this point we have the resources to formulate the following analysis:

(B) S is omnipotent at t in W if and only if for any state of affairs p, if there is a world W^* such that
(i) W^* shares the same history with W at t, and
(ii) at t in W^* someone actualizes p,
then S has the power at t in W to actualize p.

Though this analysis is surely appealing, we believe that it is nonetheless inaccurate. Its insufficiency can be traced to one primary deficiency: such an analysis fails to take account of the way in which the free actions (and dispositions to free action) of other beings would necessarily limit the power of any omnipotent being. Let us now show how this limitation arises.

As noted above in our discussion of actualization, there seems to be good reason to think that the libertarian analysis of freedom is correct. If so, it follows that not even an omnipotent being can causally determine the free actions of another agent. This fact, of course, was what accounted for the distinction between strong and weak actualization, a distinction which allows that a being can bring about a state of affairs in two distinct ways.

However, if libertarianism is true, it has a second and equally significant impact on the analysis of omnipotence. To see this, let us imagine the following situation. Suppose that at a time t a nonomnipotent being named Jones is free with respect to writing a letter to his wife. In that case Jones has the power at t to actualize

    (7) Jones's freely deciding at t to write a letter to his wife,

and he also has the power at t to actualize

    (8) Jones's freely deciding at t to refrain from writing a letter to his wife.

From this it follows that there is a world W, sharing the same history with our world at t, such that at t in W someone (viz., Jones) actualizes (7); and it also follows that there is a world W^*, sharing the same history with our world at t, such that at t in W^* someone (viz., Jones) actualizes (8). So given (B), any agent who is omnipotent at t in our world must have at t both the power to actualize (7) and the power to actualize (8).

However, on the assumption that libertarianism is true it is fairly easy to show that no one distinct from Jones — not even an omnipotent agent — *can* have at t both the power to actualize (7) and the power to actualize (8). Let C stand for the circumstances in which Jones finds himself at t. If libertarianism is true, then C includes the fact that there is a temporal interval beginning before t and including t, in which there is no causally sufficient condition either for Jones's deciding at t to write the letter or for his deciding at t not to write the letter. But now consider the following counterfactual:[16]

    (9) If Jones were in C at t, he would freely decide at t to refrain from writing a letter to his wife.

Like any proposition, (9) is either true or false. Furthermore, since (9) tells us what Jones would do if left free in a certain situation, no one other than Jones can simply decide to make (9) true or false, for no one other than Jones can determine how Jones would *freely* act. Therefore, not even an omnipotent being can decide by himself to make (9) true or false; its truth-value is something he is powerless to affect.

The consequence of this inescapable powerlessness is that, regardless of whether (9) is true or false, there will be a state of affairs which, despite meeting the conditions set down in (B), cannot be actualized at t by any being other than Jones — even if that being is omnipotent at t. For suppose (9) is true. In that case, even an agent who is omnipotent at t does not have the power at t to actualize (7). He cannot, of course, strongly actualize (7), for he cannot causally determine Jones's acting freely in a certain way. But neither can he weakly actualize (7). He can, perhaps, arrange things so that Jones is in C at t. But if he does so arrange things, then (9) tells us that Jones will freely refrain from writing the letter and thereby actualize (8) rather than (7). On the other hand, if (9) is false, then our omnipotent agent cannot at t weakly actualize (8). The most he can do in an attempt to bring about (8) is to bring it about that Jones is in C at t. But if (9) is false, then it is *not* the case that if Jones were in C at t, he would strongly actualize (8). And no one weakly actualizes (8) unless Jones strongly actualizes it. So if (9) is in fact false, then not even an omnipotent agent has the power at t to actualize (8).[17]

Therefore, whether or not (9) is true, there will be some state of affairs satisfying the conditions specified in (B) which even an omnipotent agent is incapable of actualizing. And since this inability results solely from the *logically necessary* truth that one being cannot causally determine how another will freely act, it should not be viewed (as (B) does view it) as a kind of inability which disqualifies an agent from ranking as omnipotent.

It follows, then, that an adequate analysis of omnipotence must acknowledge the logically inescapable limitations which counterfactuals such as (9) would place on an omnipotent agent. Now it should be obvious that there are many counterfactuals which, like (9), tell us how beings would freely act. In fact, since there are presumably an infinite number of circumstances in which a being can find himself, there will be an infinite number of such counterfactuals for any free agent. Nor can we limit our consideration exclusively to *actual* free beings. For though an omnipotent agent might well have the power to create free beings who are not now actual, he would nonetheless be limited by the counterfactuals relating to the free actions of these beings as well. Hence, our analysis of omnipotence must recognize the importance of counterfactuals of freedom regarding not only *actual* beings but *possible* beings as well. If we believe that, strictly speaking, there are no possible but non-actual beings, we can make this last point by saying that the relevant counterfactuals relate not to individuals but to *individual essences*, where P is an individual essence if and only if P is a property which is such that (i) in some possible world there is an individual x who has P essentially and (ii) there is no possible world in which there exists an individual distinct from x who has P.[18] An individual x will thus be said to be an *instantiation* of individual essence P just in case x has P.

Now suppose we call a complete set of such counterfactuals of freedom a *world-type*. If the law of conditional excluded middle were true — i.e., if it were the case that for any propositions p and q, either p counterfactually implies q or p counterfactually implies the negation of q — then a world-type could be defined as a set of counterfactuals indicating, for every individual essence and every possible set of circumstances and times in which it could be instantiated and left free, how an instantiation of that essence would freely act if placed in those circumstances.

However, many philosophers reject the law of conditional excluded middle, for they feel there are at least some cases in which p counterfactually implies neither q nor its negation.[19] Hence, it would probably be wiser for us to provide a more general definition of a world-type which does not presuppose the truth of this law. Let us say, then, that a world-type is a set which is such that for any *counterfactual of freedom* — i.e., any proposition which can be expressed by a sentence of the form "If individual essence P were instantiated in circumstances C at time t and its instantiation were left free with respect to action A, the instantiation of P would freely do A" — either that counterfactual or its negation is a member of the set. (To obviate certain esoteric technical problems, we might also stipulate that for any two members of the set, the conjunction of those two members is a member of the set as well.) Let us also say that a world-type is *true* just in case every proposition which is a member of it is true. (Since we are assuming an exact isomorphism between propositions and states of affairs, we may take a world-type to be, alternatively, a set of counterfactual states of affairs.)

Now any free being will have some say in determining which world-type is true. For example, since Jones is free to decide whether or not to write that letter to his wife, it is up to him whether the true world-type includes (9) or its negation. However, the vast majority of the counterfactuals which go to make up a world-type relate to beings other than Jones, and Jones, of course, is powerless to make such counterfactuals true or false. So for any free agent x there will be a set of all and only those true counterfactuals of freedom (or true negations of such counterfactuals) over whose truth-value x has no control. Since such a set will clearly be a subset of the true world-type and will be characteristic only of x, let us refer to it as the *world-type-for-x*.[20]

So it is a necessary truth that every being is in a sense simply presented with a set of counterfactuals whose truth-values he is powerless to control. That is, for any agent x the world-type-for-x will remain true regardless of what x does. So it is logically impossible for x to bring about any state of affairs which is inconsistent with the truth of the world-type-for-x with which he happens to be confronted. That is, it is logically impossible for him to bring about any state of affairs which does not obtain in any world in which that world-type-for-x is true. And since it is also logically impossible for any agent to escape this type of limitation, we cannot allow such a limitation of power to disqualify a being from ranking as omnipotent. Hence, if we allow "Lx" to stand for the true world-type-for-x, then x should not be required, in order to rank as omnipotent, to possess the power to actualize any state of affairs that does not obtain in any world in which Lx is true. We can consider this as our fourth condition for an adequate analysis of omnipotence.

So the power of any being x will necessarily be limited by the set of counterfactuals of freedom which constitute the true world-type-for-x. Moreover, since these counterfactuals do relate to the *free* actions of agents, none of them will be logically necessary truths. Even if (9) is true in the actual world, it could not be a necessary truth, for Jones could not be free regarding letter writing if there were no world in which he does decide to write in the circumstances in question. So though the true world-type-for-x (where x is distinct from Jones) in our world may include (9), there are other worlds in which the true world-type-for-x includes the negation of (9). Hence, different world-types-for-x may be true in different worlds. And this gives further support to the claim, made above, that an analysis of omnipotence must be relativized to a possible world.[21]

5. If our first four conditions of adequacy were pedantically specific, our fifth and final condition is refreshingly vague. Simply stated, it is that no being should be considered omnipotent if he lacks the kind of power which it is clear an omnipotent agent ought to possess. Such a requirement might appear redundant at this point. However, it is actually needed to rule out an analysis like the following, which satisfies our first four conditions:

> (C)　S is omnipotent at t in W if and only if for any state of affairs p and world-type-for-S Ls such that p is not a member of Ls, if there is a world W^* such that
> (i) Ls is true in both W and W^*, and
> (ii) W^* shares the same history with W at t, and
> (iii) at t in W^* S actualizes p,
> then S has the power at t in W to actualize p.[22]

Instead of furnishing us with an analysis of absolute maximal power, the right-hand side of (C) merely provides an analysis of the maximal amount of power that can be had at t in W by *any being with S's nature*. As such, it may be satisfied by a being obviously lacking omnipotence, e.g., the infamous Mr. McEar. To avoid this result we will satisfy our fifth condition by insisting that to count as omnipotent, a being should have the maximal amount of power consistent with our first four conditions.[23]

II

Though we are aware of no previously offered analysis which satisfies each of these five conditions, it seems to us that an acceptable analysis of omnipotence can be formulated. For consider:

> (D)　S is omnipotent at t in W if and only if for any state of affairs p and world-type-for-S Ls such that p is not a member of Ls, if there is a world W^* such that
> (i) Ls is true in both W and W^*, and
> (ii) W^* shares the same history with W at t, and
> (iii) at t in W^* someone actualizes p,
> then S has the power at t in W to actualize p.

(D) appears to satisfy each of our desiderata. It is stated in terms of actualizing states of affairs and does not presuppose that an omnipotent being would have to strongly actualize every state of affairs he brings about; in other words, it leaves a place for weak actualization. The inability of even an omnipotent being to actualize necessarily unactualizable states of affairs is acknowledged by (iii), while his inability to change the past is recognized by (ii) and (iii) together. Furthermore, by employing the notion of a world-type-for-S, (D) satisfies our fourth condition. And, finally, (D) requires that an agent who is omnipotent at t in W have the power to actualize *any* state of affairs (other than a member of Ls) which *any* agent actualizes at t in *any* world satisfying conditions (i) and (ii). Consequently, it seems to us that (D) does provide a philosophically adequate analysis of maximal power.

(D) also appears to be immune to the so-called paradoxes of omnipotence. Suppose that Sam is omnipotent at t in our world. Does (D) require that Sam have the power at t to actualize the state of affairs

> (10)　Its being the case that there will be a stone which Sam, though he exists, cannot move?

The answer depends upon what further properties Sam has. If Sam is essentially omnipotent, then he cannot at t actualize (10). But (D) does not require that he have this power, since in that case (10) is a logically impossible state of affairs and thus not possibly such that anyone actualizes it. On the other hand, if Sam is only contingently omnipotent, then (D) might well require that he have the power at t to actualize (10). But there is no paradox here. By actualizing (10) Sam would merely bring it about that at some future time he will be nonomnipotent.[24]

Again, take the following state of affairs:

> (11) Its being the case that a completely uncaused event will occur.

Does (D) require that Sam have the power at t to actualize (11)? If one can actualize (11) only by causing the event in question, then (D) does not require that Sam be able to actualize (11). For in that case it is logically impossible for anyone to actualize (11), even if (11) is a logically contingent state of affairs. On the other hand, if (11) is possibly actualized by someone, then Sam must have the power at t to actualize it. In neither case is there a paradoxical result.

But what of this state of affairs:

> (12) Someone is actualizing p, and Sam, though omnipotent, is not actualizing p,

where p is a state of affairs which even nonomnipotent agents can normally actualize? Must Sam have the power at t to bring it about that (12) will obtain? One might have doubts about whether it is logically possible for any agent to actualize (12). However, anyone who holds a fairly liberal position with respect to the diffusiveness of power might plausibly contend that it is logically possible. For instance, a nonomnipotent being could bring it about at t that (12) will obtain at t^* by bringing it about that he will be actualizing p at t^*, when in fact it is true that Sam will not be actualizing p at t^*. But then, by the same token, it appears that Sam too may have the power at t to bring it about that (12) will obtain at t^*. Sam would do this by bringing it about that he will not be actualizing p at t^*, when in fact it is true that someone else will be actualizing p at t^*.

Of course, it is plausible to think that if Sam is an essentially divine (i.e., eternally omnipotent, omniscient, and provident) being, then he weakly or strongly actualizes at any time t every state of affairs (other than a member of the true world-type-for-Sam) which *anyone* actualizes at t. In that case Sam would never have the power to bring it about that (12) will obtain. But neither would any other agent ever have this power in any world containing an essentially divine being. So (D) would not in this case require that Sam have the power at t to bring it about that (12) will obtain. In short, (12) seems to present no serious problem for our analysis of omnipotence. Perhaps there are other states of affairs which would present a problem, but we have not been able to think of any.

Furthermore, our analysis has not been "corrupted" by theological considerations. Indeed, (D) appears to be quite neutral with regard to what additional properties an omnipotent being might conceivably have. Given (D), there is no obvious conceptual requirement that an omnipotent agent be eternal, necessary, essentially omnipotent, uniquely omnipotent, omniscient, or morally impeccable — a being could conceivably lack any or all of these attributes at a time t in a world W and yet still be omnipotent at t in W. Of course, for all that (D) tells us, an omnipotent being could equally well possess any or all of these attributes (leaving open for now the question of moral impeccability, which will be discussed below). In short, it appears that (D) neither requires nor forbids an omnipotent being to possess the theologically significant properties mentioned above and thus does exhibit the kind of independence from religious matters which we would presumably prefer our analysis to exhibit.

III

So it appears that (D) meets our conditions for philosophical adequacy. But what of its theological adequacy? Does (D) allow the traditional religious believer to consider God both omnipotent and incapable of acting reprehensibly? That is, does it permit one to evade the Geachian abandonment of divine omnipotence without endorsing the Pikean rejection of divine impeccability?

In attempting to answer these questions, we would perhaps be well advised to begin by noting that, given our analysis of omnipotence, there is no conceptual problem with an omnipotent agent's being impeccable. For though our analysis does apparently require that an omnipotent being have the power at a given time t to actualize many evil states of affairs, e.g.,

(13) An innocent child's being maliciously tortured,

it does not require that our omnipotent being also possess omniscience at t. Indeed, it does not require that he be very knowledgeable at all. He could conceivably be utterly ignorant of the consequences of his actions and hence bring about evil states of affairs such as (13) unintentionally. Provided that his own ignorance is not a state for which he is himself culpable, it would seem to follow that he could not be held morally blameworthy for those evil states of affairs which he might unintentionally actualize at t. Hence, the ability to actualize such states of affairs at t does not entail the ability to act in a morally reprehensible fashion at t. The possibility of an omnipotent but impeccable being is thus left open by our analysis.

Of course, this demonstration of the compatibility of omnipotence and impeccability lends little assistance to the traditional theist who professes belief in a God who, in addition to possessing both of these attributes, is omniscient as well. How, one might ask, could an impeccable God who knew with certainty the ramifications of any action he might take have the power to actualize evil states of affairs such as (13)?

Troubling though such a question might appear, it would seem that our analysis provides the theist with a rather obvious response, a response which should sound familiar to those conversant with theistic replies to the atheological argument from evil. The analysis of omnipotence which we have proposed does not require an omnipotent being to have the power to *strongly* actualize states of affairs like (13); the ability to *weakly* actualize them is sufficient to satisfy the conditions laid down by (D). Once this is recognized, it no longer appears strange to contend that God, while remaining impeccable, might well have the power to actualize a state of affairs such as (13). For (13) could be part of some world W which is itself such that God's actualizing it might be morally justifiable. Perhaps the actuality of (13) in W leads to greater good than would have occurred had (13) not obtained; perhaps it leads to less evil. In any event, it is surely conceivable that God recognize that his allowing one of his creatures freely to torture an innocent child would as a matter of fact result in a world so good that this allowance was morally acceptable — and this despite the fact that the actual torturing would remain an evil state of affairs and the torturer would remain blameworthy. Hence, since even an impeccable God could have the power to weakly actualize worlds such as W which contain moral evil, and since in actualizing such worlds he must weakly actualize the evil states of affairs such as (13) which they contain, it follows that God can indeed remain impeccable even though he has the power to actualize evil states of affairs.

Now it might be thought that this response is still inadequate. It might be thought that there are some states of affairs which are *so* evil that *no* possible world containing them is a world that anyone could be morally justified in actualizing. Hence, since no divine being could ever have the power even to weakly actualize these states of affairs, no such being could rank as omnipotent. (We are willing to accept the assumption, made by this objection, that a being who is divine at *t* at least weakly actualizes any state of affairs [other than a member of the true world-type-for-him] that is actualized by anyone at *t*.)

Though this objection might well be potent against the theist who views Yahweh, the person who is in fact God, as a contingently divine being, it lacks efficacy against one who holds the more traditional belief that Yahweh is an essentially divine — and so essentially impeccable — being. For on this view no state of affairs of the sort just described obtains (or, consequently is actualized by anyone) in any possible world in which Yahweh exists. Hence, (D) does not require that in order to be omnipotent Yahweh must ever have the power to actualize any state of affairs which is necessarily such that anyone who even weakly actualizes it is morally reprehensible for so doing. In fact, if we go one step further and adopt the Anselmian claim that Yahweh is a necessary being as well as an essentially divine being, it follows that no such state of affairs obtains (or, as a result, is actualized by anyone) in *any* possible world. Some such states of affairs might be *conceivable,* but they are not, according to the Anselmian, *logically possible.*[25]

However, even for the Anselmian, Geach's challenge to the notion of an omnipotent God remains to be met. If God is essentially impeccable, there is no world in which he fails to fulfill a promise he has made. But if this is so, does it not follow that by making a promise God limits his ability to act in the future and thus renders himself less than omnipotent?

It appears at first that we have a straightforward answer to this question, viz., that by making a promise to his creatures God indeed limits his power, but not in a way which compromises his omnipotence. For suppose, to use one of Geach's examples, that God has already promised that Israel will be saved.[26] And assume that from this it follows that God does not now (at *t*) have the power to actualize

(14) Its being the case that Israel will never be saved.

Can we conclude, given (D), that God is not now omnipotent? A close look at (D) reveals that the answer to this question is negative. For in any possible world which shares the same past with our world at *t*, an essentially divine being who is essentially incapable of breaking his promises has promised prior to *t* that Israel will be saved. So in every such world Israel is saved. Hence, no one actualizes (14) at *t* in any such world. So (D) does not require that in order to be omnipotent now, God must now have the power to actualize (14).

This solution to Geach's problem is extremely attractive, and if all else should fail, we will resort to using it. However, we can adopt it only if we abandon the account sketched above of what it is for two worlds to share the same history at a given time. For on that account the state of affairs

(15) God's promising that Israel will be saved

is nonimmediate, since it entails the future-tense proposition that Israel will be saved. Hence, (15) is not a member of any submoment, i.e., it does not count as part of what is temporally independent at the time at which it obtains. And from this it follows that a world *W* might share the same history (in our sense) with our world now at *t* even if (15) has already obtained in our world but never obtains prior to *t* in *W*. So given our official interpretation of condition (ii) in (D), it may very well be the case that in order to be omnipotent, God must now have the power to actualize (14). But this seems to entail the theologically odious conclusion that God now has the power to break a promise and so is not impeccable.

Still, we are reluctant to scrap our explication of what it is for two worlds to share the same history at a given time, and this reluctance itself is in part motivated by theological concerns. For our explication of this notion allows us to avoid the deterministic claim that if

(16) God's believing (the future-contingent proposition) that Israel will be saved

now obtains, then it is now no longer within the power of the children of Israel to lead, without exception, lives heavily laden with moral turpitude. Rather, we can say that God's present belief that Israel will be saved is temporally dependent on the fact that the children of Israel will freely accept his grace and live accordingly.[27] So it is conceivable that (16) never obtains in a world which shares the same history with our world at the present moment t, since in that world God believes at t that the children of Israel will freely reject his grace and choose to separate themselves from him.

Of course, philosophers have devised other, non-Ockhamistic, strategies for dealing with the problem of foreknowledge and freedom. Some argue in effect that (16) is a logically impossible state of affairs, either because a future-contingent proposition can be neither true nor false, or because — as Prior would have it — a future-contingent proposition expressible by a sentence of the form "It will be the case that p" cannot be true.[28] However, if one accepts this way out of the deterministic problem, then it seems to follow that (15) is logically impossible as well. For it obtains at a time t only if it is *true* at t that Israel will be saved. So on this view one cannot make sense of the central religious claim that God makes promises (or gives assurances) which in some way or other guarantee the truth of contingent propositions about the future.

Geach himself employs the alternative tactic of claiming that statements ostensibly about the future are really about present intentions, dispositions, tendencies, or trends.[29] So (16) obtains just in case God believes that things are presently tending toward Israel's salvation. But this is compatible with the freedom of the children of Israel, since they may by their free actions reverse this trend, in which case at some future date (before the Judgment) it would turn out to be true that Israel will not be saved. Their freedom is preserved, however, only at the expense of the traditional belief that God now knows exactly what will happen at every future moment. It is sufficient, Geach contends, that God, like a grand chess master, knows all the possible moves we might freely make and also knows exactly how he would counter each of those moves in order to accomplish his purposes.[30] Nevertheless, it is difficult to see how an orthodox Christian can accept this emasculation of the notion of divine providence. Like the promise to save Israel, many of God's promises seem to presuppose foreknowledge of exactly how his creatures will freely act. Once we deny such foreknowledge, as Geach does, then we open up the possibility that God makes promises which he will not and cannot fulfill. For even Geach insists that God cannot cause his creatures to act freely in the way he desires them to act. And suppose that they all freely reject his grace. Will he than save them? Will his kingdom then come? The answer, it is clear, is no. But if God does not have foreknowledge, then he cannot discount this possibility when deciding what to promise. The grand chess master cannot accomplish his purpose if, unbeknown to him, his opponent will refuse to move according to the rules or will simply decline his invitation to play. So, given Geach's view, either God cannot in good conscience, as it were, promise that Israel will be saved — which is false according to faith; or it is logically possible that God's promise to save Israel go unfulfilled — which is also false according to faith.

So our disinclination to abandon a broadly Ockhamistic account of divine foreknowledge stems in large part from a consideration of the theological consequences of the alternative accounts. Now it may be, of course, that even within an Ockhamistic framework one could find some acceptable reason to count (15) as immediate while counting (16) as nonimmediate. For perhaps it is plausible to think that while God's beliefs about the future depend on what will happen, his promises with respect to the future are by contrast efficacious. However, we can see at present no way to formulate a general account of immediacy which preserves this asymmetry between God's promising and God's believing without producing other unacceptable consequences — especially in cases like (15) where God promises to actualize future-tense states of affairs whose actualization depends in part on the free actions of his creatures. Moreover, there are theological reasons for thinking that God's beliefs about the future are in some sense or other causally efficacious.

Instead of pursuing this line of inquiry, we will close with a very tentative sketch of an alternative strategy for reconciling, within the parameters of our Ockhamistic account of sharing the same history, God's omnipotence with his impeccability.

But we wish to reiterate that if this strategy turns out to be irremediably defective, then we will jettison our account of what it is for two worlds to share the same history at a given moment. In that case the previously noted "straightforward" response to the promising problem would, at the cost of some vagueness in our analysis of omnipotence, become available to us.

Now it is not unreasonable to think that some of God's promises to us reflect necessary truths about how God treats his creatures. For example, perhaps it is a necessary truth that any sinful free creature whom God creates is offered divine forgiveness. Suppose that this is so, and suppose further that God has promised that Jones, a sinful free creature of God's who now exists, will be offered divine forgiveness. Given this scenario, even though the state of affairs

(17) God's promising that Jones will be offered divine forgiveness

is nonimmediate, it is still the case that there is no possible world W sharing the same history with our world at the present moment t such that at t in W someone brings it about that Jones will never be offered divine forgiveness. For in any such world Jones is a sinful free agent created by God, and so he is offered divine forgiveness. Let us call promises of this sort God's *standing* promises. It should be obvious that (D) does not require that God ever have, in order to be omnipotent, the power to break a standing promise.

It is also reasonable to believe that many of God's promises to us reflect at least in part his beliefs about how he and his free creatures will freely choose to act in the future. For instance, his promise that Israel will be saved presumably depends in part on his belief that the children of Israel will, under the influence of grace, freely act in the ways appropriate for their salvation. And perhaps his promise never again to destroy the world by flood reflects his knowledge of his own present, but constant, intentions and hence his foreknowledge of his own future free actions. Let us call promises of this sort God's *conditioned* promises.

Now suppose that God's promise to save Israel is indeed a conditioned promise, and suppose that he has already made this promise. Since (15) is nonimmediate, it may follow from our account of omnipotence (given the Ockhamistic construal of condition [ii] in [D]) that God now has the power to bring it about that Israel will never be saved. Suppose that this does in fact follow. Does it follow further that God has the power to break a promise or to act in a morally reprehensible way? The answer, it should be clear, is no. For take a world W which shares the same history (in our sense) with our world now at *t* and in which Israel is never saved. Since in W God knows that the children of Israel will reject his grace, he never promises in W that Israel will be saved. So it is compatible with all the assumptions made above that there is no possible world in which God breaks a previously made conditioned promise. That is, even if God now has the power to bring it about that Israel will never be saved, it does not follow that God now has the power to act in a way which is such that if he were to act in that way, he would have broken a promise. For if he were to bring it about now that Israel will never be saved, then in those possible worlds most similar to ours in which Israel is never saved, God never promises to save Israel — where the relevant notion of two worlds being similar at *t* is at least partially defined in terms of the notion of two worlds sharing the same history at *t*. (We are, for present purposes, assuming a standard possible-worlds account of the truth conditions for counterfactuals.)

While this line of thought admittedly requires further elaboration and defense, we believe that even this brief sketch shows it to have some merit. If some such account of God's promises is indeed correct, then to complete our argument we have only to add the claim that necessarily, any promise made by God is either a standing promise or a conditioned promise. Since neither of these types of promises undermines the claim that God is both omnipotent and impeccable — or even the stronger claim that God is both essentially omnipotent and essentially impeccable — our analysis of omnipotence does not succumb to 'Geach's objection even if (D) is construed Ockhamistically.

Hence, we conclude that (D) does provide the type of analysis of the concept of omnipotence which Geach and Pike held to be impossible. The theist does not *need* to choose between divine omnipotence and divine impeccability. And neither, fortunately, does God.[31]

NOTES

1. Peter Geach, *Providence and Evil* (Cambridge, 1977), p. 4. The chapter entitled "Omnipotence" first appeared as an article by the same name in *Philosophy* 48 (1973): 7-20.

2. Nelson Pike, "Omnipotence and God's Ability to Sin," *American Philosophical Quarterly* 6 (1969): 208-16. In fairness to Pike we should point out that he distinguishes three senses of the claim that God cannot sin: viz., (a) that it is logically impossible that someone both is God and sins; (b) that the person who is God is incapable of sinning; and (c) that the person who is God "cannot bring himself" to sin even though he is capable of sinning. Pike accepts (a) and (c) but rejects (b) as incompatible with the claim that the person who is God is omnipotent. Our response is that (b) expresses the correct understanding of the claim in question — and it is (b) which we hope to show, *pace* Pike, to be compatible with the claim that the person who is God is omnipotent. Later we will endorse the stronger, Anselmian thesis that the person who is God is *essentially* incapable of sinning, which again, given our analysis of omnipotence, is compatible with that person's being omnipotent. Hence, we admit Pike's contention that God is not morally praiseworthy for not sinning. But we hasten to add that God is still morally praiseworthy, since he performs many supererogatory acts, e.g., sending us his only begotten Son.

3. Jerome Gellman contends that *omnipotence* should be explicated in this way, so that an omnipotent agent is one who has all the power that an essentially perfect being can have. See Jerome Gellman, "Omnipotence and Impeccability," *The New Scholasticism* 51 (1977): 21-37. In support of this analysis Gellman argues for the dubious thesis that omnipotence is conceptually inextricable from the other properties (e.g., impeccability) a perfect being must have. In effect, then, he assimilates omnipotence to almightiness. By contrast, in *The Coherence of Theism* (Oxford, 1977), pp. 158-61, Richard Swinburne admits that God cannot be omnipotent in the strongest sense, but he goes on to claim, *pace* Geach, that it is perfectly appropriate to use the term 'omnipotent' in a weaker sense in which omnipotence is compatible with impeccability. We believe that these moves made by Gellman and Swinburne are undesirable and, as we will argue, unnecessary.

4. To the best of our knowledge, McEar makes his first contemporary appearance in Alvin Plantinga's *God and Other Minds* (Ithaca, 1967), pp. 168-73. But a similar difficulty was recognized at least as early as the later Middle Ages. For instance, the following note

was added by an anonymous writer to one of the manuscripts of Ockham's *Ordinatio* I, distinction 42: "Nor is a being said to be omnipotent because he can do all things which are possible for him to do . . . since it would follow that a minimally powerful being is omnipotent. For suppose that Socrates performs one action and is not capable of performing any others. Then one argues as follows: 'He is performing every action which it is possible for him to perform, therefore he is omnipotent'." See Gerald Etzkorn and Francis Kelly, eds., *Ockham: Opera Theologica*, vol. 4 (St. Bonaventure, N.Y., 1979), p. 611.

5. See Alvin Plantinga, *The Nature of Necessity* (Oxford, 1974), pp. 172-73.

6. Plantinga's discussion of weak actualization is in the place cited in note 5. Chisholm's discussion occurs in *Person and Object* (LaSalle, Ill., 1976), pp. 67-69. (Chisholm takes as basic the concept of causally contributing to a state of affairs rather than the notion of actualizing a state of affairs.) It is no mean feat to formulate an exact analysis of weak actualization, but an intuitive grasp of this notion will suffice for our purposes in this paper.

7. For some analyses of omnipotence *not* stated in terms of actualizing states of affairs, see Richard Francks, "Omniscience, Omnipotence and Pantheism," *Philosophy* 54 (1979): 395-99; Jerome Gellman, "The Paradox of Omnipotence, and Perfection," *Sophia* 14 (1975): 31-39; and (though less explicitly) J. L. Mackie, "Evil and Omnipotence," *Mind* 64 (1955): 200-12.

8. We say "at least some," since those who espouse an Ockhamistic response to the problem of future contingents might want to insist that we can have the power to actualize certain "future-infected" past-tense states of affairs. See Alfred J. Freddoso, "Accidental Necessity and Power over the Past," *Pacific Philosophical Quarterly* 63 (1982): 54-68.

9. Despite what we have said, it may be the case that Descartes is an offender rather than just a trivializer of our second condition. See Harry Frankfurt, "Descartes on the Creation of the Eternal Truths," *Philosophical Review* 86 (1977): 36-57.

10. This condition on power, despite first appearances, is consistent even with compatibilism. The compatibilist would, however, deny the libertarian claim that we can add the further condition that W and our world continue to share the same laws of nature (with no violations) at t itself.

11. See, for instance, Jack W. Meiland, "A Two-Dimensional Passage Model of Time for Time Travel," *Philosophical Studies* 26 (1974): 153-73; and David Lewis, "The Paradoxes of Time Travel," *American Philosophical Quarterly* 13 (1976): 145-52.

12. For a dissenting view cf. Dennis M. Ahern, "Miracles and Physical Impossibility," *Canadian Journal of Philosophy* 7 (1977):

71-79. Our own inclination, on the other hand, is to believe that laws of nature specify the causal powers or dispositions of natural substances. Hence, such a law, e.g., that potassium has by nature a disposition to ignite when exposed to oxygen, might remain true even when the manifestation of the disposition in question is prevented solely by the action of a supernatural agent.

13. See Alfred J. Freddoso, "Accidental Necessity and Logical Determinism," *The Journal of Philosophy* 80 (1983): 257-278. This paper argues for our account of sharing the same history on purely philosophical grounds rather than on the theological grounds suggested below.

14. A state of affairs p may be said to entail a proposition q just in case it is logically impossible that p obtains and q does not. And p may be said to involve q just in case p is necessarily such that whoever conceives it conceives q.

15. Many recent philosophers have failed to recognize explicitly that any being's power is necessarily limited to states of affairs which are "temporally contingent." In addition to Francks, Gellman, and Mackie, see George Mavrodes, "Defining Omnipotence," *Philosophical Studies* 32 (1977): 191-202; Nelson Pike, "Omnipotence and God's Ability to Sin"; and Richard Purtill, *Thinking about Religion* (Englewood Cliffs, N.J., 1978), p. 31.

16. Throughout this essay we shall follow David Lewis's practice of not presupposing that the term "counterfactual" is to be applied only to conditionals with false antecedents. See David Lewis, *Counterfactuals* (Cambridge, Mass., 1973), p. 3.

17. The argument here is little more than a variant of Alvin Plantinga's argument against the thesis that God must have the ability to actualize any possible world. See Plantinga, *The Nature of Necessity*, pp. 180-84.

18. The definition of an individual essence is taken from Plantinga, *The Nature of Necessity*, p. 72.

19. For a discussion of conditional excluded middle see Lewis, *Counterfactuals*, pp. 79-82. We wish to note in passing, however, that even if the law of conditional excluded middle is false, there may be a weaker analogue of that law which is true and would be sufficient for our present purposes if we chose to invoke it. For the antecedents of the counterfactual conditionals which concern us here are all of the form "Individual essence P is instantiated in circumstances C at time t, and P's instantiation is left free with respect to action A." Now suppose we stipulate that the substituend for "C" must be a complete description of the past at t along with a clause specifying that the same laws of nature continue to hold at t. In that case there seems to be good reason to believe that where p is a proposition expressed by a sentence of *this* form, then for any proposition q, either p counterfactually im-

plies q or p counterfactually implies the negation of q. However, a complete defense of this position is impossible here, and so we will proceed on the assumption that there is no acceptable version of the law of conditional excluded middle.

20. The relationship between the world-type-for-God and divine freedom is discussed at length in Thomas P. Flint, "The Problem of Divine Freedom," *American Philosophical Quarterly* 20 (1983): (forthcoming). One terminological point suggested there might also be noted in passing here: God's knowledge of the world-type-for-God is identical with what is generally referred to as God's *middle knowledge.* The Molinist thesis that God has middle knowledge of contingent propositions whose truth-values he cannot control is hotly contested in traditional theological discussions of grace, providence, and predestination. We cannot pursue the matter here but simply wish to note our belief that it is only by adopting some version of Molinism that one can preserve a suitably strong understanding of both (a) the doctrine of divine providence and (b) the thesis that human beings are free.

21. Among authors discussed previously, Francks, Gellman, Mackie, Pike, and Purtill all fail to satisfy this fourth condition. In addition see Gary Rosenkrantz and Joshua Hoffman, "What an Omnipotent Agent Can Do," *International Journal for Philosophy of Religion* 11 (1980): 1-19; James Ross, *Philosophical Theology* (Indianapolis, 1969), p. 221; and Douglas Walton, "Some Theorems of Fitch on Omnipotence," *Sophia* 15 (1976): 20-27.

22. The stipulation that p not be a member of Ls is required if we assume that by their free actions agents actualize the corresponding counterfactuals of freedom. In the example used above, this assumption would amount to the claim that by actualizing (8) Jones also actualizes (9). If, on the other hand, we deny that a counterfactual of freedom can properly be said to be actualized by anyone, then the stipulation in question is, though superfluous, completely harmless. So we have added it just to be safe.

23. Despite Richard Swinburne's protestations to the contrary, the conceivability of McEar disqualifies his analysis. See Richard Swinburne, "Omnipotence," *American Philosophical Quarterly* 10 (1973): 231-37. For much the same reason an analysis offered tentatively by Plantinga must also be deemed unacceptable. On this analysis a being S is viewed as omnipotent at time t in world W if and only if (1) there are states of affairs S can strongly actualize at t, and (2) for any state of affairs p such that there is a possible world which shares the initial world-segment prior to t with W and in which S at t strongly actualizes p, S can at t strongly actualize p.

24. This response to the stone paradox conforms to that given by Rosenkrantz and Hoffman in "What an Omnipotent Agent Can Do."

25. The Anselmian response to Pike was first formulated by Joshua Hoffman in "Can God Do Evil?" *Southern Journal of Philosophy* 17 (1979): 213-20.

26. In his comments on this essay William Wainwright argued that if our account of freedom is correct, then God cannot make promises like the alleged promise to save Israel. For a "promise" of this sort would be such that God could not fulfill it on his own, as it were, since he does not have the power to determine causally the free actions of his creatures. At best, Wainwright contends, God could (in virtue of his foreknowledge) "assure" some creatures that they would be saved. But he could not "promise" this. We are not completely convinced by this argument, since it may be that God, in virtue of his knowledge of the future free acts of his creatures, can make promises where nonomniscient beings can only give assurances. But even if Wainwright is correct, it seems that an orthodox believer could comfortably construe talk of God's promises as talk about God's assurances, at least in those cases where free human actions are involved. Indeed, as Wainwright himself notes, we often give assurances by using the expression "I promise you that . . . . " One who is sympathetic to Wainwright's argument should simply construe our talk below of "conditioned promises" as talk about assurances.

27. We acknowledge that this way of speaking is infected with (some might say "infested" with) Molinist assumptions about the relation between grace and freedom. See note 20 above.

28. See A. N. Prior, "The Formalities of Omniscience," in *Papers on Time and Tense* (Oxford, 1968), pp. 26-44.

29. Geach, *Providence and Evil*, ch. 2, esp. pp. 44-54.

30. The image of God as a grand chess master, first popularized by William James in his essay "The Dilemma of Determinism," is in many ways reminiscent of Jacques Maritain's image of God as an almighty stage manager who incorporates our improvisations into his providential play. See Maritain's *God and the Permission of Evil* (Milwaukee, 1966), p. 79. "The Dilemma of Determinism" is found in William James, *The Will to Believe and Other Essays in Popular Philosophy* (New York, 1897, 1956), pp. 145-83.

31. We wish to thank William Wainwright, our commentator at the conference, along with Nelson Pike and Philip Quinn for their helpful comments on an earlier version of this essay.

Creation II

JAMES F. ROSS

Introduction

I continue what Anthony Kenny (1979: 10 and 121; see my review, Ross, 1982B) insists is impossible: to state traditional doctrines about the power, knowledge, unchangeability, and goodness of God while avoiding logical conflict with the temporality of the world and human freedom or making God blameworthy for the wrongdoing of humans. The particular obstacle here is a certain cosmological incoherence and naivete that has been introduced into philosophical theology recently.

Kenny's book does not address my earlier analysis of the extent of God's power (as effective choice over every contingent state of affairs *ad extra*) (Ross, 1969 and 1980A and 1980B) or my argument that a negative moral character cannot warrantedly be attributed to God on the basis of the observed evil in the world, no matter what the world is like (Ross, 1969 and 1980A, ch. 6). More recently than Kenny's book, I argued further ("Creation," 1980B)[1] (i) that a logical conflict between God's all encompassing power and human freedom simply does not emerge from the considerations offered by Plantinga and others, (ii) that God's determining which *possible* world is actual entails his immutability and eternity for his creating,[2] and (iii) that God's creating the universe does not require but actually *excludes* any change in God, even though something else, or nothing at all, might have been created instead.

Those steps, I believe, withstand Kenny's objections. So why can we not complete my task by directly addressing other issues that Kenny makes central, about how God knows indexically situated things (like what time it is now), or future contingencies not yet determined in their causes (like whether you will stay interested in this paper), or how God appears historically and geographically within creation, issuing commands and promises? The really serious difficulties do not lodge, where Kenny thinks they do, in the analysis of those issues. They lie in inventing adequate analogies and articulating an underlying metaphysics to support a different *picture* of God's relationship to the universe that will, as a by-product, resolve those issues and be cosmologically coherent. By treating (i) states of affairs as parasites (ontological) of real beings, (ii) causation of states of affairs as equivocal with causation of being, and (iii) metaphysical causation as different from, but presupposed by, nomological causation, I shift the picture of God's relationship to the world to one that is cosmologically literate and obviates the usual paradoxes about creation, freedom, foreknowledge, and determinism. For instance, it emerges that God caused it to be so that Adam sinned, but not in a sense of "cause" univocal with its token in "Adam was the cause of his own sin." Similarly it is true, but only denominatively and/or metaphorically true, that God knows the future. Absolutely nothing is literally future to God, and real time is created with matter.

So here I look further at God's power, the causation in creation.

I. Causation in Creation

The nature of God's power is not the same as its *extent*. It is the power to cause being. (See Aquinas, *S.T.*, 1a, 45, 6c; *S.C.G.*, 2, 15, 5.) That has to be distinguished from what it accomplishes as a logical consequence (determining the actual state of affairs), the way perceiving visually is the object of the power of sight, but knowing certain things is a logical consequence of its successful exercise.

My definition of omnipotence (1969 and 1980A:221; "Creation," 1980B:14) as "effective choice over all extrinsic contingent states of affairs" specifies the *extent* of God's power in these respects, by opposing theories that exempt some contingent states (say human choices) from almighty power and entail that God does not determine which, among possible worlds, is the actual one. Further, the predicate "effective," used to characterize the choices of an omnipotent being, indicates another *extent* of God's power: that it is *unthwartable* because there is no possible world where God wills something that does not obtain or where something (extrinsic to him) obtains contingently that he does not will. (This "possible worlds" talk is continued here subject to the *extensive* qualification forthcoming in my book *Creation* [University of Notre Dame Press].)

(i) To say there is a logical equivalence between God's effective willing and every extrinsic contingent state of affairs is not to explain the *nature* of that power. It is at most to specify its extent by *stating the range of states of affairs* it comprehends.

Conversely, every contingent extrinsic state of affairs (for instance, my choosing to go on a journey or my accidentally falling) is logically equivalent to some state of God's effective willing. But none compels, produces, or accounts for God's willing. Specifying the range of God's power in terms of the ontological *shadow* (the states of affairs) of real beings is useful, but, heedlessly reiterated, it can be greatly misleading, as we will see.

(ii) Second, God's will is unthwartable in that whatever he wills (in any possible world) happens and nothing happens that he does not will. That is still in the "shadow vocabulary" and provides no *explanation* of God's power. For *my* will is unthwartable by God: there is no possible world in which I do something at will and God wills that I do not. Yet, my will does not compel, produce, or explain God's. Logical equivalence, and thus entailment of states of affairs, is simply *not* a relevant kind of compulsion to create any of the standard puzzles about autonomy and human freedom. This is a central point implicitly misunderstood in typical discussions.

(iii) Third, the fact that what God *does not* will in any possible world is what he wills *not* to obtain (his "not-willing-that" is the same as his "willing-that-not") is the *transparency* of his will over states of affairs *ad extra*. Again, stated in the shadow vocabulary: every state of affairs included in a given world is transparently willed by God, and not merely included, as when *I* act or move. This, again, is a description of God's power in terms of the *logical outcome* of what he does directly and underivatively: cause being. There is no "totality of states of affairs," no maximal set of actual contingent states of affairs that God causes to obtain, directly. In fact, there is no set-theoretic totality at all.

(iv) The replacement picture is this: creation is a universal transcosmic force, constant, invariant, whose entire *effect* is the *being* of everything and every other force that there is, and whose entire effect *might* have been the being of whatever else is merely possible. Creation, creative *force*, *is* God, not something added or a contingent modification or state of God; it is God's very being. No matter what had been actual, that force would have been unchanged. Had a different cosmos been created, that force would not have been different, but only God's election among his incompossible effects.

For God to *elect* one cosmos instead of another (or none) could not require that at some hypertime God had "not yet" made a choice and was "foreseeing outcomes" (see Ross, 1980B:620-22, and 1982B); that would be contradictory.

Nothing in the divine nature requires this election, but only *some* election because not all states of affairs are compossible: for instance, the seventy or so *universal* physical constants might have had an infinity of other values but could not have more than one (if universal and invariant) in a given cosmos (Diem and Lentner, 1970:228-29). Logically, no matter how God actually elected, *without* a prior time or state of *not* having so elected, he still might have elected otherwise, the reality ("realization") of the "otherwise" lying *entirely* in the effects, just as I might have thought of something else this minute, not by a difference in any before, but entirely by a difference in what I think of at this moment. Thus, "choice" and "election" function to explain why *this* cosmos instead of (but not "in preference to") some other and, derivatively, that other possible worlds might have been actual had God elected differently. The "insteadness" of God's electing is manifested and realized entirely by what there is, regarded in *contrast* to what might have been. (See sect. VI on God's reasons.) God's *being* causes the realization of his election, as sunlight causes radiant heat, and as light causes objects to be visible, totally and continuously dependent. "Hunc autem effectum causat Deus in rebus, sicut lumen causatur in aere a sole quamdiu aer illuminatus manet" (*S.T.*, 1a, 8, 1).

That is the summary picture. Next, let us consider whether, even in nature, there is more than one kind of causation.

II. Metaphysical Causation, Though in Nature, Contrasts With Nomological Causation

There are kinds of causation, different enough to exhibit different senses of "cause."

(i) Nomological explanations derive *outcomes* from *antecedents* by quantified *laws*; for instance, changes of gas pressure from changes of its temperature. "Antecedent conditions plus law entails outcome." Such laws are usually regarded as regularities, sometimes even *necessities*, of transaction, transformation, transmission, or correlation. Such causation is everywhere in the cosmos. Yet, it everywhere presupposes another kind of causation, the kind by which structures and "inner mechanisms" *produce* the observable behavior of things, constitute the very things that "behave."

Metaphysical causation, the causing of being, is not generating outcomes from antecedents through intervening or overarching laws. There is *no* transaction, transformation, transmission, or correlation. It is constant causation, instantaneous, but not by an inner mechanism because the outcomes are not conceptually necessitated by the description of the "inner mechanism."

(ii) Among nomological causes the *concept* of the outcome — say, increased pressure — does not include the thing (or sort of thing) that is the cause, e.g., increased temperature. Such laws are conceptually synthetic if there is real causation and not just theoretical inclusion. The same effect (as a change of measured quantity) could be produced in other ways, e.g., by compression of the volume (with consequent temperature rise). Presumably, that (sort of) effect is logically possible without that (sort of) cause, the cause is possible without that effect, and both "effect" and "cause" are possible when not in that relation.[3]

One physicist, David Bohm (1957:14), thought that although effects at the molecular level do not in their correct scientific description *conceptually include* the statement that they have such atomic causes (or the reverse), in fact, such causation is a posteriori (i.e., to be discovered by experience alone), necessary, and "bound up with the basic properties of the thing which help define what it is" (1957:14). The macroproperties (behavior) of water may be impossible without its microstructure, molecularly and atomically and the reverse, as well; but the conceptual inclusion is "downward" only, if there is any at all.

In contrast, *metaphysical* causes "include and are included in their effects." There is a *semantic* relationship between adequate (scientific) descriptions of *what* the cause and effect are, *as well as* a logical relationship among the things or states of affairs to which these descriptions apply. The metaphysical effect (as a *sort*), adequately conceived, includes its cause.[4] If you really understand dreams, their dreamer-dependence will be semantically included in an adequate scientific description of what a dream is.

(iii) As David Bohm commented, all the particular events and things that are causes of effects separated in space-time are subject to "Newton's law that action and reaction are equal. From this law it follows that it is impossible for any one body to affect another without itself being affected in some measure." Metaphysical causes *never* satisfy that condition. No equal and opposite reaction, no transaction, transmission, transformation, or concomitant variation, is to be found. (Cf. Aquinas, *De pot.*, 3, 7, and *In 3 phys.*, 4.)

(iv) Metaphysical effects are never separated by any space-time interval from their causes as are the typical event-sequences explained by scientific law. Again, just the reverse. The metaphysical cause is "everywhere" in its effect, and its causing is coextensive spatiotemporally with the being of the effect, the way that crystal geometry is everywhere in the crystal it forms.

(v) The expression "metaphysical cause" applies analogously to whatever really accounts for being (vs. happening). A metaphysical cause can be an *extrinsic producer* of the effect, as a thinker is of his thoughts, or an *extrinsic exemplar*, like the DNA formula for humans, provided it has an intrinsic physical realization in a thing. An abstract structure, e.g., defective crystal structures (e.g., Frenkel Defect, Schottky Defect), accounts for empirical dispositional properties of the piece of steel so structured. It *causes* the steel to behave macroscopically, empirically, as a thing so structured molecularly as to exhibit those defects, yet not in the sense of "causes" in which an impurity dropped into the molten metal can "cause" the defect. It *causes* the steel to be a certain kind whose law-like behavior can be explained as "on account of the defective crystal structure" which itself is abstract, subject to mathematical description and not dependent for its reality upon having material realizations (as is an abstract particular, like a given symphony).

Metaphysical causes *intrinsic* to a thing, e.g., the formal structure of wave theory (VN, 1958:1979), can typically be realized in many materials, say, water, other liquids, compressed air, radio signals (and, possibly, gravitational waves). Both the organization (structure) and the material (say, freon) so structured are *intrinsic* causes (real, explanatory factors) of the being of the physical thing (the sound wave, gas wave, or water wave) that results.

Mathematical structures (geometrical, topological, etc.) molecularly realized, e.g., certain crystal structures, *account* for spatial, shape, and volume relationships among sugar particles and for whether light and radio waves pass through equally in all directions. The structure, without which the crystal cannot exist, is a cause of its being *what* it is (a certain kind of crystal).

However, the structure is only (imperfectly) *realized* by the component molecules (whose electrical bonding instantiates the structure); it is not a *part* (component) of the crystal (as is a molecule). One reason for this is that the structure is everywhere in the crystal, and other crystals "have" the same structure. Even if a molecular inner mechanism (e.g., the "bonding" electrical force) explains how the molecules *take on* the overall structure and why *certain* atoms make diamond crystals, and others, copper or arsenic crystals, that still does not obviate the explanatory role of the abstract, formal crystal structure which determines *what* it is that we have (e.g., a certain *kind* of crystal which will have, say, the property of passing current in one direction and not in the other, or unequally in the two directions) and other properties that are consequences of the abstract form.

Similarly, the logical structure realized in the circuitry of my pocket calculator makes it a *calculator* rather than, say, a *diatonic harmonizer* (which similar logical circuitry in the same kind of stuff can realize). Thus, structure, which is a universal, of course, is a partial cause of a being. Portions of water, air, or light realize certain formal structures (at least to a high approximation and regularity of consequent behavior) that *make* them to be a *wave* or a *vortex*. (The stuff of which the calculator, wave, or cone is made also accounts partially for the thing's being a calculator or wave.)

The stuff-structure co-causation appears at physical dimensions from 10^{-12} centimeters (diameter of the atomic nucleus) to 10^{28} centimeters (radius of the observable universe) and for objects of a mass 10^{38} grams (mass of an average galaxy) to 10^{-24} grams (mass of an electron). The stuff-structure analysis seems to provide each "next-included" physical dimension (to a given one) with the role of "inner mechanism," where the behavior of its components "explains" their *collectively* realizing an abstract structure that governs, produces, or even *constitutes* the behavior at the macro-level. For instance, 6,000 or so assorted atoms structured properly will make a protein molecule. "Protein molecule," as an abstraction, is itself a nested structure within higher life forms. How the component-behavior "explains" the macro-behavior varies. Sometimes it is by "necessity" based upon the conceptual inclusion of each, adequately described, in the other (theoretical inclusion or reduction); sometimes by "synthetic necessity" that we have, supposedly, discovered in experience; and sometimes by brute causation, production, that we cannot yet further explain.

No account of causation I know of is even plausible. So we will have to get along now with a limited analysis that may be just reliable enough to disclose the presence in nature of at least another kind of causation from that supposed in the nomological conception of natural causes.

There is causation that is not event-causation directly but instead is causation of being. Where the causing-of-the-cause *is*, in some respect, the being-of-the-effect, we have metaphysical causing. As D. Burrell said, explaining Aquinas on causation (1979:133), "Whatever is itself *in act* in the relevant respect need not do anything further to be a cause." Where the causing is continuous, not separated in space-time, where cause and effect are of different sorts (e.g., an abstract structure and an individual thing), and where a proper scientific description of the effect semantically (conceptually) includes its having that kind of cause of being, we have metaphysical cause and effect.

On this account, *emergent* properties are empirical manifestations at physical dimensions $N+1$ of abstract formal structures that are realized by instantiation of their constants and variables at the next "inner-mechanism level," N, by physical entities (say atoms in a protein molecule) which themselves realize at level N abstract formal structures, instantiated by physical entities at $N-1$ (the subatomic particles) in the same way, by instantiating variables and constants. (I hope to refine this notion in the future.) Whether this relationship of structure within structure is recursive, and so endless, I am not sure. I conjecture that it is and that it was the absence of a way of talking about infinitely nested structures that left Aristotle's theory of "prime matter" unconvincing.

On this view there is no prime matter. God creates *whole* beings, from the "top down," each of which involves infinitely many nested formal structures. The beings are not "built up" by adding structure, just as an infinite sequence is not constituted by counting. Rather, the structures nest as necessary for the realization (in matter) of the overall form of the thing.

(vi) *Metaphysical effects are* entia ab alio. R. Chisholm (*Person and Object*, 1976:51, 105, and elsewhere) distinguished "ens per se" from "entia per alio" (sic),[5] developing the notion of an "ontological parasite" that "never is or has anything on its own." I refashion Chisholm's contrast between *ens per se* and *ens ab alio* for the present inquiry. The cosmos is not a parasite (see Ross, 1982A, and Quinn, 1979:289-302); neither is it an *ens per se* in the sense that either Aquinas or Spinoza considered God to be. It is an *ens ab alio*, a thing from-another. Within the cosmos there are substances, people, for instance, that are "from-another" but not "of-another."

There are ontological parasites, things we can make true statements about but such that those truths can be "paraphrased" away into (cf. Chisholm, 1976:51) truths about other things in the role of "host." These are things about which we can "make clear that the truth of the sentence [purportedly referring to such things][6] is compatible with the non-existence of such an object," just as Chisholm provided. (Cf. Chisholm, 1976:107.) For instance, De Tocqueville's trip; yesterday's fear;

Hume's mistakes. The cosmos or universe (unlike "the actual world") is not such a parasite.

Not all things that are "*from* another" are "*of* another," and not everything "of another" is so in the same way or for the same reasons. "*Ens ab alio*" subdistinguishes into (i) *ens ab alio with absolute existence*: things produced by something else and continuously dependent, like you and me and cells and stars, but not "*of* another": things *metaphysically dependent* (see below) but not *inherent* in another or *mere consequences* of another; and (ii) *ens ab alio with real inesse*, like the shape of my face, the color of my eyes, meanings, paintings, model-years, administrations. These are *inherent* and thus dependent in being *and of another* but not "reducible" in being. None of these is an ontological parasite because none has a "collapsible quiddity." That is, none is such that *what*-it-is is conceptually derivative from *what* it is *from*.

The second group (inherent, dependent but not reducible beings) can be further divided because the *inesse* of properties or characteristics, *inherence*, is not the *inesse* of *parts* (nose, eyes) which *compose* things. And that is different again from the *inesse* of the microparts, which compose things transiently and, when replaced, do not affect the individuation or kind. Lastly (iii) there are the things that are *ab alio without real inesse*, the parasites whose entire being is *per aliud*, as Chisholm explained.

Any metaphysically dependent thing is *ab alio;* its being is impossible unless caused by something of a different kind, by a cause not of the same "species" as the effect.

One thing metaphysically depends upon another of type F (and, so, is an effect of it) just in case: (a) it exists and it could not be at all unless "accounted" for by another of type F; (b) it is not "reducible" to the other (as the ontological parasite is to its host); (c) it is quidditively "out of" and/or "because of" another(s); (d) its standing in the same dependence relation throughout its being is a necessary condition of its being at all; and (e) all possible things of the same kind are similarly dependent upon the same kind(s) of producing and conserving causes. (This is intended only to approximate because the phenomena are analogous; for instance, dreamer, dream; wave-structure, wave.)

Among *beings* some *are* absolutely and are not *of* something, even though they are *from* something or *out of* something. You and I are *out-of* flesh and blood, organs, systems, cells, molecules, atoms, and so forth. And we are "from something" both in nature (ancestors) and metaphysically, a creator. We are also "because of another," a structure or organization of matter that necessarily yields humans. But we are not, as are our faces and gestures, merely "of something." Intrinsically, because of the stuff-structure relationships and the real essence-individual relationship, and extrinsically, because of the dependence of all contingent beings, we are *entia ab alio*. No account of creation that "fudges," fails to explain, or excludes that fact will be satisfactory. Views of creation as a kind of making propositions true or states of affairs obtain are anemic.

III. God's Causing Is Metaphysical. Its Object Is Being

Creation is a universal force, like a light that causes things to be (visible), but which would have been unchanged had other things been caused to be (visible) instead. From God's understanding — to make some purely conceptual distinctions — the election, but not production, of things flows. God is a radiant force, present everywhere, throughout everything that actually is, even throughout the gravitational writhing of otherwise empty space (if there is any) and, therefore, throughout physical space-time itself, causing it to *be*. Aquinas said:

> Since God is being itself through his own essence, created being has to be his proper effect, just as the proper effect of fire is to ignite things. (Cum autem Deus sit ipsum esse per suam essentiam, opportet quod esse creatum sit proprius effectus eius: sicut ignire est proprius effectus ignis.) (S.T., 1a, 8, 1)

> Therefore God is the cause of being for all things. (Deus igitur est causa essendi omnibus aliis.) (S.C.G., 2, 15, 5)

> So no thing whose essence is not its being exists by its essence; rather it exists by participation in something, viz., in being itself. . . . But what exists by participation in something cannot be the first being. For that in which something participates in order to exist is prior to it. (Nulla igitur res cuius essentia non est suum esse, est per essentiam suam, sed participatione alicuius, scilicet ipsius esse. . . .

Quod autem est per participationem alicuius, non potest esse primum ens: quia id quod aliquid participat ad hoc quod sit, est eo prius.) (*S.C.G.*, 1, 22, 8-9)

Aquinas' example of fire suggests that the proper effect of a thing is what it brings about by acting in virtue of *what* it is, rather than, say, by virtue of some adventitious quality or incidental condition, like its location, occupation, or age. The produced is, if determined by *what* the producing thing is, the producer's proper effect. The proper effect of God, who is being, is the being of things. What the creature lacks, without God's causation, and receives is participation in *what* God is, being, to-be. (One can see why Aquinas followed Plato and called the relation *participation*. . . . I acknowledge that we do not understand this part plausibly, as yet.)

IV. God's Causing Is Analogous to Other Kinds of Metaphysical Causing

God's causing is *analogous* to a number of other kinds of production: the production of thoughts by thinkers, dreams by dreamers, characters by authors, structured things by abstract structures. They are all "production," "causation," but the word differentiates (analogously) to accommodate to contrasting semantic neighborhoods.

You cannot infer from the fact that the same words apply that the same truth-conditions hold for the statements expressed, or from the fact that a certain condition holds for one case that the same condition holds for another. In fact, where the common expressions are analogous, you can infer quite the opposite: no matter how many truth-conditions obtain in common (for instance, a whole set of conditions for metaphysical dependence of the effects, see Ross 1980A:254-56 and xxxii and xxxv), there must still be a difference of truth-conditions and, more particularly, a difference of meaning-relevant truth-conditions (Ross, 1982A:178), say between efficient and formal causes. A truth-condition for a statement S is meaning-relevant just in case its not holding for a statement S', expressed in the very same words, *marks* a difference of *linguistic meaning* in one or another common word. Thus, the fact that "The men are late today," used for different statements, Monday and then Tuesday, has different truth conditions is not enough for a difference of meaning-relevant conditions or a linguistic meaning-difference (Ross, 1982A:196).

To object that the relationships of characters to authors and of creatures to God cannot be metaphysical dependence because creatures have moral relationships to God while characters do not to their authors (see Gutting, comments for APA, December 1980) misses the point that these are *analogous productions* of *entire* being; they are not the same.

I labor over this because the mistake has been made over and over again and receives its most vitiating use when God's "causing" states of affairs to obtain is treated as univocal with God's "causing" certain things to be. Oakes (1977), Gutting (1980), Griffin (1973), and others thought that because I say God, minds and authors produce effects that are metaphysically dependent upon them, I must be arguing that creating things is nonmetaphorically a kind of dreaming, imagining, or authoring them. So, they say, the creatures would not have an adequate measure of either reality or freedom in such a case. None of that, of course, follows at all.

God's causing is *analogous* to authoring, composing, singing, inventing, dreaming, imagining, and thinking up. It is analogous to other kinds of production we have not noticed yet, too. Analogous, in that it is production of things in their entirety and in complete and continuous dependence in being. But it is not, nonmetaphorically, any of those things. It is *not* alike in the mode of being of the products, just as the other examples differ among themselves in the mode of being of the *causes*.

I have said that God's causing is analogous to an abstract mathematical structure's (wave) causing because of the *entire* and continuous dependence of the individual wave upon its having that structure. Yet God is not the form or intrinsic structure of things. (God's causation is efficient causation of being, not formal causation.) I have said God's causation is like a light producing radiant heat, like lasers producing holograms, in the continuous and entire dependence really *distinct* of the effect and in the absence of any need for changes in the cause to produce the effect. I have said God's causing is like the universal force of gravity in that it is realized everywhere, throughout space-time and throughout all physical being, without any change. Still, creation is not a force *in* nature: it is the cause *of* nature.

God's causing being can be analogous to many diverse things without even possibly being the same as any one of them. Nothing is exactly the same as anything it is analogous to (for a near-synonym of the one predicate has to fail to apply that way to the other). "Produce," "cause," "create," and "make" apply analogously across the cases of metaphysical dependence (and other kinds of causation as well). There is no justification whatever for anyone's reasoning from the fact that the effects are categorically different from one another to the conclusion that the causation involved cannot be analogous.

V. Creation and Human Freedom

I conjecture that Plantinga and Kenny think that in creating by acts of will God *actualizes states of affairs.* Plantinga speaks, in my opinion, incoherently of "initial segments of possible worlds." Though he distinguishes creation from actualizing states of affairs (1974:169), he gives as his reason why God cannot actualize his own being omnipotent that "he does not create himself" (169); for, as with properties, "to suppose that they have been created is to suppose that, although they exist now, there was a time at which they did not" (169). Does that mean that for any state of affairs involving existence, God's actualizing it is "to suppose that although they exist now, there was a time at which they did not"? Then God could not actualize the actual world, create time and space, or make all things. Others, like Geach, who largely follows Aquinas (though introducing the grand master of chess into the issues of foreknowledge and predestination), portray God as a *maker* whose whole product, the cosmos, is like a clock or other ingenious device, invented by God but working on its *own*, with God, as it were, holding it on the shelf of being.

But creation is neither of those ways. The being of the cosmos is like *a song on the breath of a singer.* It has endless internal universal laws, and structures nested within structures, properties that are of *the song* and *not* of the singer or the voice or the singer's thought, though produced by them and attributively predicated of them: for example, intervalic distances and progressions, mathematical patterns (say inversions), rhythmic and metric patterns, and the more elusive but still real musical properties of "drive," "intensity," "color," "lyricality," and "beauty" (all of which might belong to a Bach aria faithfully croaked by a frog).

Created being is continuing being. Like songs, things are for-a-time; they take time in being, in fact, have being through time. (Though that kind of time does not pass.) There are no instant material things (though some are very "short," some for 10^{-29} second). So every cell, atom, forcefield, and galaxy is continuously depending, as if it were the massed sounds from a small orchestra of God's intentions, the product of intersecting beams of light of many frequencies, separated by God's holding a simple prism of intentions up to the pure light of his being (perhaps, as with Leibniz, the "most simple" prism).

The universe is continuously depending, like a song or a light show (cf. *S.T.*, 1a, 8, 1); its being is its own, yet it is from a cause, everywhere, and at no *including* time. The song is thought out: the substantial beings are produced, like the component tones, and only derivatively are all the formal structures they satisfy realized, and do the states of affairs obtain. To talk about the world primarily as "states of affairs" is like talking about things by inference from their shadows. With a complex enough shadow-science it might be done but at great loss.

I do not find it coherent to analyze existing throughout a given interval of time as "existing *at* every included instant," even with added qualifications. So, to analyze continuous creation as creation of a persisting thing *at* every instant included in the time it persists (see Quinn:1983) is, again, "shadow talk" because "creates" is explained as a relationship of God to a state of affairs, namely, that God brings it about *that x exists at t*. But if we treat "exists-at-*t*" as an undecomposable monadic predicate for each *named* temporal instant, then in order that *any* such predicate apply to *x*, *x* must antecedently *be* — that is, existing at *t*, for a given *t* is not *essential* to anything, but *being* is, even though it is of-the-essence only of God.

Thus, the time that passes is internal to the universe the way it is to a musical composition (or dance). But the time which is the precondition for change is an abstract structure realized physically by the relationships among the universal constants. God is, of course, not within time and is entirely independent of it.

These analogies motivate a different picture of God in relation to the cosmos and the human will. God produces, for each individual being, the one that does such and such (whatever it does) throughout its whole time in being. Still, God is not the *agent* of the sun's motions. Nor, strictly speaking, does God cause the sun to move. Those motions of which you are *agent* (e.g., your gestures) are *your* motions; whereas those motions you produce but are not the agent of are still your effects. God does not move the sun; he makes the *moving sun to be*. So the movements of the sun are God's effects, even though he does not move it.

Similarly, God does not make the person act; he makes the so acting person *be*. Now we cannot deny, if we countenance talk about states of affairs, that if God causes the moving sun to be, he also "brings about" or "causes" its moving as it does, the states of affairs that obtain, and so, derivatively, he can be said loosely to cause the motions that are the constituents in such states of affairs. But this is "erector-set" philosophizing. One starts off with the innocent, mundane truth that God causes the moving sun to be, and, with the toys of logic and the states-of-affairs vocabulary, one *derives* statements of the form "God causes the sun to move as it does." The equivocations on "cause" are undetected and almost harmless until the same device is applied to Adam.

God causes Adam, acting exactly as Adam actually does, to *be*, not like a woundup toy that ricochets off objects in a path undetermined by the player, but to *be* wholly, including being *able* to do otherwise than as he actually does. So we go on to say "God brought it about that, caused it, that Adam freely sinned." Then we derive "God caused Adam to sin." Taking "causes" to mean anything beyond the logical by-product of the *real* causing by which Adam is made to be turns infelicity into absurdity.

The way we usually talk of God's willing that I do such and such, and of my freely doing such and such, treats the ontological shadow as the reality. States of affairs, e.g., *that* I do such and such, are ontologically posterior to being, even to my being a such-and-such doer. The "states of affairs" that I used to describe the *extent* of God's power (in the fashionable "states-of-affairs" and "possible-worlds" jargon) are only the logical epiphenomenon of the real being of God.

Does God's necessary and sufficient causation extend to my *whole* being, through time, even to my accidents and, therefore, to whatever I do freely? Absolutely. The whole physical universe, all of it, is actively caused to be. Still, to say that freedom or human agency is thereby impeded is absurd. Nothing can be or come about unless caused to be by the creator. So the fact that God's causing is necessary for whatever happens cannot impede liberty; it is a condition for it. Similarly, in no way is our liberty impeded by the fact that God's causing is sufficient for the being of the very things that do the very things that we do. Nothing possible can be impeded by its necessary conditions.

That can be nicely illustrated from Chisholm's analysis of agency (*Person and Object*, 1976:62). For a person to be "free" at a certain time "to undertake" some action there has to be a time period that includes that time and starts before it, during which there is "no sufficient causal condition either for his undertaking or for his not undertaking." He has to have doing *p* within his power.

When we analyze "causal condition," we find that it includes only *physical* necessities, causation in nature; in fact, it includes only "event-causation" and not natural metaphysical causation (but that is a minor matter to supplement). In sum, Chisholm says, "If a state of affairs is directly within an agent's power, then something he is free to undertake is such that his undertaking it would bring about that state of affairs."

There is nothing about my account of God's continuous causation and presence throughout the physical universe that suggests or implies that humans do not have a wide range of the agency that Chisholm describes. And, as I mentioned in the earlier paper (1980B:617), any condition of "avoidability" that has yet been coherently formulated and is plausibly necessary for free action is also satisfied by this account of God's causation.

Sufficiency: Things can be "overdetermined." Your being inter-
rupted in your thinking might induce anger, and your just concluding "I fouled it up again" might at the same moment also
induce anger: either alone would be sufficient.

If there can be "simultaneous" sufficient causes of the same
kind (say cognitive states of the agent), why cannot there be
logically ordered sufficient conditions of different kinds? If
there were, would either be sufficient without the other's obtaining? Not if they are logically ordered, and each implies the
other. In those free acts that I perform my will is a sufficient
condition of my acting, on the tacit condition that I continue
to *be* long enough to act, and *that* is *not* within my power to
bring about. God's "choosing that I freely write philosophy" is
not sufficient for my doing so, except on the condition that I,
in fact, do so. That is still in the "shadow vocabulary." Directly, God's making Adam, the man who first defies God, is sufficient only if Adam, in fact, does so. For a sufficient condition
to be sufficient every necessary condition's being fulfilled is
necessary.

The distinct conditions I have in mind cannot be temporally
related to one another. Further, sufficiency is relative to the
kind of story that is being told. Relatively to event-causation in
nature human action cannot consistently have lawlike sufficient conditions in prior physical events. But no account of
human freedom can be correct that so defines it that God cannot cause there to be a certain agent that does one thing rather
than another. For the being, in its entirety, is *ab alio*.

The alleged "inconsistencies" and invasions of "autonomy"
are unsubstantiated and fail to recognize what a creator creates: whole beings that are, like songs, temporal entities (and
not *entia successiva*, like Theseus's ship). God did not make
Adam to be the first man to defy God; God made Adam, who
was the first man to defy God, to be. God made Adam, who
undertook to sin. (And the latter relative clause is restrictive.)
God did not merely make Adam begin to be; he made that very
being-through-time that is Adam's. What, then, of the following reasoning?

Would the actual world have been a different possible world
had Adam not sinned? Yes (as the verbal custom is now), for
the complete actual state of affairs would have differed. Does

God determine, by causing all other being, which possible world is the actual one? Yes. Could God determine which possible world, containing Adam, is actual without determining either that Adam sins or that Adam does not sin? No. But if God determines that Adam sins, then Adam does *not* sin (because you cannot sin if you are caused to do what you do by another). So God cannot be a sufficient cause of the actuality of a possible world in which Adam sins. Thus, God did not determine which is the actual world.

There is a determining of things that is a mere logical consequence of what you do, as when you step forward to make a point, and in logical consequence, make it true that "2 + 2 = 4, and you stepped forward to make a point." There is the determining of physical events, where given the antecedent and the laws, the outcome is settled: you drop the lighted blowtorch into the gasoline-soaked rags on your boat engine. There is the determining of things within our power to do: whether to sit through a lecture or leave. There is the determining of things within our power to cause: to cough, whisper, and squirm until you have distracted everyone.

That reasoning supposes that God makes the "core" of Adam (some seem to think a being is a laminate of *properties*, e.g., Plantinga [1974:75, 77-81]), who, like a clock, runs on the mainspring of God's will but otherwise ticks on the hairspring of choice, settling for himself what he does and becomes. If God's will were to settle whether Adam sins, it would invade and cancel Adam's doing that for himself. Yet to determine causally which possible world is actual — that is what God would have to do. Here the causation is imagined to terminate in states of affairs in which individuals have *properties* (see Plantinga, 1974:51 and 151).

I urge a different picture, insisting among other things that states of affairs are not, except analogously, parasitically, and loosely, *caused* at all. There is only one kind of causation that God exerts as creator, and that is to cause *being*. In consequence, the contingent actual states of affairs obtain. But that is parasitic causation. God "determines" the universe by making the *things* that do what they do, including all the free things able to do otherwise, that could have done otherwise but will never *be* in a world in which they do anything other than what they actually do in this one. (Please do not entertain the fancy that Adam ever exists, has real being, in a world where he does anything other than as he did.) God makes all the free things that do *as* they do, instead of doing otherwise as is in their power, by their *own* undertaking. So God does not make Adam sin. But God makes the sinning Adam, the person who, *able* not to sin, does sin. The action is the creature's, but the being is from God (*ab alio*). It follows logically that if Adam had not sinned, God would have made a person who, though able to sin, did not. And, surely, God *might* have made a person who, though able to sin, did not.

It is a nonsequitur to say that because God brought about Adam who sinned, Adam could not have done otherwise. Doing otherwise was within his power, as was choosing to do otherwise as well. Having been able to do otherwise but not having done so are necessary for the Adam who existed. Had Adam done otherwise, that cosmos would still have had its being from God; it would have been the same cosmos but a different possible world. It is the whole being, doing as it does, whether a free being or not, that is entirely produced and sustained for its time by God.

So problems that arise about God's choosing that I freely do what I do freely are in crucial respects (like other problems about his knowledge of the future and ability to change the past) *artificially* generated from the surface grammar of the "shadow vocabulary" we use to describe the *extent* of God's power. The *intentional* object of God's creating is not the states of affairs in which Adam figures as a component. The transparent *intentional* object of God's creating is the *whole* being, for-*all*-its-time, that is Adam, including Adam's doings.

Could God have made Adam under circumstances where Adam would not have sinned? Of course. Otherwise Adam would not have been really *able* not to sin when he did sin, because he would not have been really *able* to do otherwise unless God could conserve his being if he were to do otherwise. Does that mean God *would* have conserved his being if he had done otherwise? Of course. For how else would Adam have done otherwise?

God's assertorical thinking is his *making* ("*cognitio Dei causa rerum*") (Aquinas, *S.T.*, 1a, 14, 8c.) His proper making is to make things *be*. So God knows, with respect to contingent things, whatever he causes to *be*. Because he causes there to be a person, Adam, who defied him, we say "he brought it about that Adam defied him"; but that is shadow talk again: he caused the *being* of a person who defies him, but the being did the defying on his own. God knows, by *making*, whatever is contingently so. (And that should not be described as requiring a set-theoretic totality of facts.)

VI. The Reasons for Creation Are the Beings Created

God *has*, in what he makes, an adequate reason for making it. Had he made something else, he would have had in *it* an adequate reason for making that. And had he made nothing at all, he would have had in his own being an adequate reason for making nothing at all. Thus far my reasoning exactly parallels St. Thomas Aquinas's. We diverge on *why*.

God's reason is the *being* that obtains as a result of his election. There is no reason for *preferring* one world *over* another. Each, were he to choose it, is completely adequate to "explain" its election; that is why they are equally possible and none is "more likely" to be actual than any other. It is not, as Aquinas argues, God's perfection that gives him a reason to create and no *need* to create, but rather the perfection of what is made is a sufficient reason for God's making it, though God's own perfection might have been a sufficient reason for not making anything else at all.

The reason there is no state of God's choosing among possible worlds for some reason (or another) is that there is no logical space for that to have gone on. It could not have been among the necessary states of affairs because whatever the reason might have been would have determined the final choice, so that all worlds would not, in fact, be really as well as logically possible. It could not have been among the contingent states of affairs because then the choice would not have determined the possible world but would have been part of it.

The purpose (objective) of creation is the *beings* caused. "Creating," understood in shadow talk as "determining the actual world," does not have a purpose because it is necessary. (Some possible world must be the actual world.) "Creating" as "causing something else to be" is abstract and has its purpose (objective) in the *particular* making which it requires, which, in turn, has as *its* purpose the beings made. The end of the explanatory chain is in the being God elects. There can be no meta-chain, as Aquinas seemed to think, where choice is the outcome of weighting merits or reasons for activity. All possible worlds have to be equally meritorious, otherwise God's perfection would be in accord with his nature but not *from* it (as Leibniz decided).

Those considerations affect the issue of "presence" by leading the imagination away from pictures where God's understanding is "located" at a distance from the cosmos, as if he were looking *out* upon prospective creation and then upon actual creation. Like the Aristotelian notion that the understanding is where *what* it understands is, not squeezed inside the skull (or heart), so too God's being is *throughout* the cosmos and everything in it; it is not *in* space-time because it is not capable of physical change.

Those who think of existence as some property or attribute added to lists of other properties to yield things, and do not regard "being" as most importantly different from any quality, will not be satisfied by this account. But just consider this difference: when we say "God *is* being itself" (*ipsum esse subsistens*), no analysis in terms of Leibnizian identity could possibly capture what is claimed: it is *not* a statement that every property of God is a property of being itself or that necessarily anything true of the one is true of the other. Rather, a contrast is offered. We say nothing else *is* its own being; all other things *have* being, and none of them are such that "what" they are is "to be." The relationship of God to the world cannot be cognitively disentangled until we reject any idea that possible worlds differ qualitatively and that actuality is something added to a world. Rather, being is communicated to *things* and the being of the created things is as continuously and immediately depending as is the message in a phone call.

Conclusion

On this analysis God is everywhere by his *being* (as well as by his exercised power and his knowledge, just as Aquinas thought). There is no point of talking, except denominatively from the creature's *imaginary* (see Aquinas)[7] viewpoint, or metaphorically of events or things being related to God in time, whether past, present, or future or according to any "before" and "after." From the most distant part of the universe, 10 billion light-years away from us (Eccles, 1979:27), that far *past* from us, to the farthest stars, further into "*our*" future than the earth will last (so that their light will never reach us), and even further *beyond our future* into the future from "*here*" — the imaginary place(s) we will have been, a "here" that *moves*, rotating around that galactic center once every 250 million years, and moves as the galaxy itself revolves "slowly" on *its* axis, all 10^{11} stars, and moves as the galaxy rushes at incomprehensible velocity away from the other galaxies — God is everywhere. Nothing could be without his causation, not even space-time. All future events on earth are forever in the past of galaxies more than 4 billion light-years away and moving further apart.

As Wheeler (1977) remarked, "But no Universe can provide several billion years of time, the minimum needed to 'cook' the heavy elements out of hydrogen according to general relativity, unless it is several billion light-years in extent." There is only an *imaginary* (as Aquinas called it, *De pot.*, 3, 1, ad 10) "now" across the universe, just as the "here" for us, relatively to the *universe*, is purely imaginary. (See Geroch, 1978.) The internal time of the cosmos (given a fixed speed of light) is a function of its size. Eccles and Wheeler (1977) conjectured that the immense size of the universe is a function of its providing the conditions for the emergence of life and that a universe of 10^{11} stars (one galaxy) would last one year! Sir Bernard Lovell (1977) holds the same view. (Still that sounds self-contradictory to me, because 10^{11} stars have to be at least 100,000 light-years across, and surely nothing can last less than its extent in light-years.)

God's causation is, as I said, entirely realized in created beings, each of which is (among the things of the cosmos) for a time. And just as the causation by an abstract form is throughout the thing formed (both spatially and temporally), so the causation of the thing's being is throughout the thing's being, spatially and temporally, spread out in space-time with it. The causation is not "timed" or "tensed," only the being, in relation to other beings. It is denomination, relative naming, to transfer such predicates to God (and in some cases it is metaphor: "God is here"). God's omnipresence, as the immediate cause of being, is a direct consequence of the nature of his power: to cause being.

That frees us from the anemic metaphysics of possible worlds that are supposed to be made of states of affairs that may or may not be *actualized*, like programs that may or may not be being "run" on a computer by an operator "outside." That rhetoric is "shadow talk" because states of affairs can be brought to obtain or not obtain only in logical consequence upon what *real* being is or is not caused by God. And it frees us from the pernicious ontology of necessarily existing properties and individual essences that underlies the religiously, and logically, incoherent applied semantics for modal logic that has been directed to proofs for the existence of God and discussions of God's power and knowledge. (See Ross, *Creation* [forthcoming, University of Notre Dame Press].)

Talking about the existence of possible worlds is pernicious unless "exists" is parsed out as a merely logical quantifier ("for some *x*, *x* is a possible world . . . and . . . . ") that imports *no* claim to *being* at all. They are parasites of what really is.

NOTES

1. *Adding a condition for real relations.* Scott Weinstein pointed out that because a creature has to come-into-being for *any* of its relations (even relations of reason) to obtain, it will follow (on my analysis, 1980B:625) that all its relations are real relations. That consequence is consonant with what I say about God but discordant with my saying that creatures stand in two kinds of relations, one real and the other "logical, conceptual, consequential or Cambridge." So the stated conditions have to be augmented. The addition needed is that the relatum's changing (beginning to be absolutely or in some respect) that is necessary or logically sufficient for the relation's obtaining is *semantically included* in (but not synonymous with) the relational predicate. ("Conceptual inclusion" will do if one wants to avoid relativity to a certain language's vocabulary.) Thus, to be a sibling of X, A has to be conceived (or undergo the legal equivalent) by the same parents. The real change realized in A has to be part of *what is meant* by saying that the relationship obtains between A and X, and not something merely implied.

Sometimes "A is thinner than B" means in part "A weighs less than B," where A and B are people of roughly the same stature. That could happen in various ways, by A's losing or B's gaining weight. But it cannot come about by A's arms being amputated, so that A weighs less than B. The kind of real change necessary for a real relation to obtain, from the viewpoint of some relatum, is semantically included in the relation predicate. The relation is real, is "realized" in the relatum that changes that way, either as a necessary or as a sufficient condition of the relation's obtaining.

2. Further, I remind you that nothing can be omnipotent, as I define that, and exist in only some possible worlds (see Preface to 1980 printing of Ross, *Philosophical Theology*), although "existing in a possible world other than the actual" is *not* a predicate that actually obtains of anything but is only a "manner of speaking." So, if such a being is possible, it exists.

Similarly, for an omniscient being. If it is consistent to say there is a being that by its nature knows *whatever* is so (no matter what is so), then it must be true that such a being exists. For to be *able* to know whatever is so, the thing must exist "no matter what," and in all possible worlds. Because there is no serious issue of the *consistency* of such statements, there can be no serious doubt about the existence of such a being but only problems about its relationship to the cosmos.

3. Nomological causes and effects are no more than inputs and outcomes under general or universal regularities of nature. See B. Russell, "On the Notion of a Cause," *Mysticism and Logic*, 1918.

4. I speak of an "adequate scientific description" of "what" the cause and effect are because a language not developed for aligning causes of things (for explanatory objectives) may lack semantic relations of the kind supposed, and its speakers may lack the requisite concepts and conceptual relationships. Thus, a community might have no conception of authoring or being a character, even though they may enact what appear to us to be plays.

5. Professor Chisholm's expression "ens per alio" (pp. 51, 2; 104; 107; 140; 212; 215; 228) conflates two Latin expressions into an ungrammatical one; they are *ens per aliud* and *ens ab alio*. Parasites are *per aliud*; creatures are *ab alio*.

6. The bracketed expression is my insertion.

7. In *De potentia Dei*, q. 3, a.1, reply to 10th objection, Aquinas says: "When a thing is made from nothing, its being begins in an instant, and its nonbeing is not in that instant, nor is it in any real but only in an *imaginary* instant. *For outside the universe there is no real but only an imaginary dimension,* in respect of which we say that God is able to make a thing outside the universe at this or that distance from the universe; even so, *before the beginning of the world there was no real but an imaginary time,* wherein it is possible to conceive

an instant which was the last instant of nonbeing. Nor does it follow that there must have been a time between those two instants, since *real time is not a continuation* of imaginary time" (italic added). And in art. 2, corpus, he says: "there was no time when there was no world. And yet, we may find a common but purely imaginary subject, insofar as we *imagine* one common to them when there was no world and afterwards when the world had been brought into being. For even as outside the universe, there is no real magnitude, we can nevertheless picture one to ourselves: so, before the beginning of the world there was no time and yet we can imagine one. Accordingly, creation is not in truth a change; but only in imagination and not properly speaking but only metaphorically."

BIBLIOGRAPHY

Bohm, David. 1957. *Causality and Chance in Modern Physics.* University of Pennsylvania Press: Philadelphia.

Burrell, David B. 1979. *Aquinas: God and Action.* University of Notre Dame Press: Indiana.

Chisholm, Roderick, M. 1976. *Person and Object.* Open Court: Illinois.

Diem, K., and Lentner, C. 1970. *Scientific Tables.* Ciba-Geigy Ltd.: Basel, Switzerland.

Eccles, John, Sir. 1979. *The Human Mystery.* The Gifford Lectures 1977-78. Springer International: Switzerland.

Geroch, Robert. 1978. *General Relativity from A to B.* University of Chicago Press: Chicago.

Griffin, David R. 1973. "Divine Causality, Evil and Philosophical Theology: A Critique of James Ross." *International Journal for Philosophy of Religion* 4:168-86.

_____. 1976. *God, Power and Evil.* Westminister Press: Philadelphia.

Gutting, Gary. 1980. Unpublished comments on Ross, 1980B, at APA Symposium, December, Boston.

Kenny, Anthony. 1979. *The God of the Philosophers.* Clarendon Press: Oxford.

Lovell, Bernard, Sir. 1977. "A Contemporary View of Man's Relation to the Universe," cited in Eccles, 1979:32.

Oakes, Robert. 1977. "Classical Theism and Pantheism: A Victory for Process Theism?" *Religious Studies* 167-73.

Quinn, Philip. 1979. "Divine Conservation and Spinozistic Pantheism." *Religious Studies* 289-302.

_____. 1983. "Divine Conservation, Continuous Creation, and Human Action." This volume, pp. 55-79.

Plantinga, A. 1974. *The Nature of Necessity*. Clarendon Press: Oxford.

Ross, James. 1969, 1980A. *Philosophical Theology*. Bobbs-Merrill: New York; Hackett: Indianapolis.

_____. 1980B. "Creation." *Journal of Philosophy* 77:614-29.

_____. 1982A. *Portraying Analogy*. Cambridge University Press: Cambridge.

_____. 1982B. Review of *The God of the Philosophers*, by Anthony Kenny. *Journal of Philosophy* 79:410-17.

Russell, B. 1918. *Mysticism and Logic*. Longmans, Green: London and New York.

Van Nostrand's Scientific Encyclopedia (VN). 1958. D. Van Nostrand: Princeton.

Wheeler, J. A. 1977. "Genesis and Observership." *University of Ontario Series in the Philosophy of Science*. Butts, R., Hintikka, J. (eds). Reidel: Boston.

Descartes's Meditation V Proof of God's Existence

CLEMENT DORE

I

In Meditation V Descartes argues that "there is not any less repugnance to our conceiving a God (that is, a Being supremely perfect) to whom existence is lacking (that is to say, to whom a certain perfection is lacking), than to conceive of a mountain which has no valley." And he draws the conclusion that "existence is inseparable from Him, and hence that He really exists."[1]

One interpretation of Descartes's argument can be expressed thus:

(1) God is a supremely perfect being.

(2) Existence is a perfection.

So

(3) existence is inseparable from God, i.e. God really exists.

I shall assume (throughout) that Descartes is correct in claiming that existence is a perfection (and, hence, a property) or, at any rate, that it is a perfection relative to God. But even granting that premiss, the argument, thus interpreted, is unsuccessful. For nothing can be a supremely perfect being unless it exists. Hence, premiss (1) presupposes that God exists, and so the argument is, as it stands, question-begging. A non-question-begging formulation is as follows:

(1)′ *If* God exists, *then* he is a supremely perfect being.
(2)   Existence is a perfection.

So

(3)′ if God exists, then he exists.

But, of course, (3)′ is without ontological significance.

But now a much more charitable interpretation of Descartes's argument is as follows:

(1) The *concept* of God is the *concept* of a supremely perfect being.
(2) The *concept* of existence is the *concept* of a perfection (relative to God).

Hence

(3) the concept of God stands to the concept of existence as the concept of a mountain stands to the concept of a valley,[2] i.e., it is a conceptual truth that God exists.

So

(4) God really exists.

On this interpretation, premiss (1) asserts, not that *God* is a supremely perfect being, but that the *concept* of God is the *concept* of a supremely perfect being (i.e., that what we think about when we think about God is a supremely perfect being). And *that* premiss surely does *not* presuppose that God exists.

II

Still, it may look as though there is another refutation of Descartes's proof. I have the following criticism in mind: "If it is indeed the case that the concept of God (of a supremely perfect being) stands to the concept of existence as the concept of a mountain stands to the concept of a valley — or, say, as the concept of a square stands to the concept of a four-sided figure — then, *pace* Descartes, it does not follow that God really exists. For it does not follow from the fact that it is a conceptual truth that, e.g., squares are four-sided figures that there really are such objects. All that is entailed is that *if* a square exists, *then* it is a four-sided figure. (It is a conceptual truth that, say, centaurs are creatures with the torso of a human being and the hind parts of a horse, but it would surely be madness to maintain that this fact warrants us in believing that there really are such creatures. All that follows from the envisaged conceptual truth is that *if* centaurs exist, *then* they are creatures of the contemplated sort.) And, by parity of reasoning, all that follows from the claim that it is a conceptual truth that God exists is that *if* God exists, then he exists, i.e., it does *not* follow that God really exists."

But in fact this objection can be seen to be mistaken. A conceptual truth-expressing sentence is such that we can give an explanation (and, indeed, a *complete* explanation)[3] of our ability to know that it expresses a truth just in terms of the concepts which it expresses (so that our knowledge that it expresses a truth need not be based on observation). Moreover, it is the mark of a conceptual truth-expressing sentence that its being truth-expressing is explicable in terms of its expressing *precisely* the concepts which it expresses. Thus, the explanation of the fact that the conceptual truth-expressing sentence "Squares are four-sided figures" expresses a truth has to do with the fact that it is (precisely) about *squares* rather than some other objects. So the claim that it is a conceptual truth that God exists entails the claim that it is because of the concept of *God* (and not some other being) that the sentence "God exists" expresses a truth.

But suppose that "God exists" really does mean the same as "If God exists, then he exists." This latter sentence (call it "ϕ") would continue to express a truth, no matter what proper names, nouns, or definite descriptions we might substitute for "God": the envisaged sentence expresses a vacuous truth. So it is false that it is because of the concept of *God* that it expresses a truth, and, hence, false that it expresses a conceptual truth. It follows that if "God exists" really does express a conceptual truth, then it does not mean the same as the contemplated, ontologically sterile sentence ϕ. And it follows in turn that Descartes was right in claiming that the fact that "God exists" expresses a conceptual truth entails that God really exists.

It is of note that similar considerations do not apply to, e.g., "Squares are four-sided figures." Though this sentence expresses a conceptual truth, it *is* equivalent in meaning to the conditional sentence "If squares exist, then they are four-sided figures," for this latter sentence does *not* express a vacuous truth, i.e., it would express a falsehood under most substitutions of plural nouns and definite descriptions for "squares." Hence, the fact that it is because of the concept of a square that "Squares are four-sided figures" expresses a truth does not entail, in *this* instance, that it does not mean the same as the envisaged conditional sentence. However, as we have seen, things are otherwise with "God exists." This sentence expresses a conceptual truth only if it is *not* equivalent to ϕ. But now it looks as if Descartes was correct in claiming that it expresses a conceptual truth. It looks, then, as if his argument that God really exists is sound.

Here someone may wish to argue as follows: "Consider the concept of an existent winged horse. It is because of this concept that the sentence 'Existent winged horses exist' expresses a (necessary) truth.[4] But this sentence (call it "ϕ'") is surely equivalent in meaning to the ontologically sterile sentence 'If existent winged horses exist, then they exist'. Otherwise, existent winged horses (and a myriad of other such Gaunilo-type entities) really exist. But if 'Existent winged horses exist' both expresses a conceptual truth and means the same as the envisaged conditional sentence, why should not 'God exists' be taken to mean the same as ϕ?"

The answer is that the word "existent" in ϕ' functions as a (Quinean) logical particle, i.e., ϕ' expresses a logical — and, hence, vacuous — truth, since it would continue to express a truth, no matter what plural noun or definite description we might place after the logical particle "existent" (so long as the sentence ended with 'exist'). It follows that ϕ' does *not* express a conceptual truth (that it is not because of the concept of winged horses that it expresses a truth), and that is why there is no objection to the claim that it is equivalent in meaning to the ontologically sterile (and vacuous truth-expressing) sentence "If winged horses exist, then they exist."

At this point another objection may be raised: " 'God' analytically entails 'an existent, omnipotent, omniscient, and perfectly good being'. Hence, 'God exists' means the same as the vacuous truth-expressing sentence 'An existent, omnipotent, omniscient, and perfectly good being exists', which is equivalent in meaning to 'If an existent (etc.) being exists, then he exists'. But (3) of Descartes's argument is validly entailed by (1) and (2), and there is no reason to think that either of these turns out false under the present analysis of 'God'. So it is false that if 'God exists' expresses a conceptual truth, then it is not equivalent in meaning to 'If God exists, then he exists'."

One reply to this objection is that (3) does not follow from (1) and (2) as, e.g., *p* follows from *p and q*. Whether the concept of God stands to the concept of existence as the concept of a mountain stands to the concept of a valley depends in part on what "God" means. And if "God" has the meaning which is presently contemplated, then in fact it is false that the envisaged analogy holds — since it *is* a conceptual truth that mountains have valleys, but it is *not* (given the present analysis of "God") a conceptual truth that God exists. Premisses (1) and (2) should be taken as establishing a *prima facie* case for (3), but one which can be overthrown, given that the meaning of "God" is demonstrably such that it is false that "God exists" expresses a conceptual truth. (The *prima facie* case for (3) could be overthrown not only if "God" meant "an existent, omnipotent, omniscient, and perfectly good being" but if the meaning of "God" were such that God was a logically impossible being.)

But now why should it be thought that "God" does *not* mean "an existent (etc.) being"? If there is no argument to the contrary, then Descartes's argument is less than compelling. But in fact there *is* an argument which shows that the contemplated analysis of the meaning of "God" is mistaken: Let us say that for any value of X, "X has actual existence" means that the sentence "X exists" (a) expresses a truth and (b) is not equivalent in meaning to an ontologically sterile conditional sentence. Then we can rephrase Descartes's argument as follows:

(1)′ The concept of God is the concept of a supremely perfect being.

(2)′ The concept of actual existence is the concept of a perfection (relative to God).

Hence

(3)′ the concept of God stands to the concept of actual existence as the concept of a mountain stands to the concept of a valley, i.e., it is a conceptual truth that God has actual existence.

So

(4)′ God has actual existence.

Now it is plainly false that all that *this* argument establishes is the ontologically sterile conclusion that if God exists, then he exists. For what it shows, if it is sound, is precisely the opposite.

(And if "God exists" does *not* mean "If God exists, then he exists," then "God" does not mean "an existent (etc.) being.") Hence, the present argument shows that Descartes's argument is after all sound.

Here someone may say "The sentence 'God has actual existence' is equivalent in meaning to 'A being such that it has actual existence and is omnipotent, omniscient, and perfectly good has actual existence', and this sentence expresses a vacuous truth, and, hence, there is no reason to deny that it means the same as the ontologically sterile sentence 'If a being such that it has actual existence and is omnipotent, omniscient, and perfectly good exists, then it has actual existence'. Moreover, the latter sentence expresses a proposition which is compatible with its being the case that 'God exists' means 'If God exists, then he exists'. So the revised proof does not after all show that Descartes's proof has real ontological significance."

But the objection can easily be met. One reply to it is as follows: It is clear that if "God has actual existence" does not express a true proposition which is incompatible with its being the case that "God exists" means "If God exists, then he exists," then no sentence does. So my opponent is arguing in effect that the concept of God is such that it is not possible to express a true proposition which is incompatible with its being the case that "God exists" means the same as "If God exists, then he exists." But this can be seen to be wrong. Let "a C-concept" = df "a concept of something, X, such that it is possible to express a true proposition about X which is incompatible with its being the case that 'X exists' means the same as 'If X exists, then it exists'." And consider the following argument:

> (1)″ The concept of God is the concept of a supremely perfect being.
> (2)″ The concept of a supremely perfect being is a C-concept.

So

> (3)″ the concept of God is a C-concept.

Now

> (4)″ if the sentence "God has actual existence" does not express a true proposition which is incompatible with its being the case that "God exists" means the same as "If God exists, then he exists," then no sentence does.

But

(5)″ if the sentence "God has actual existence" means the same as "A being which has actual existence and is omnipotent, omniscient, and perfectly good has actual existence" (call this sentence "*S*"), then the proposition which is expressed by the former sentence is not incompatible with its being the case that "God exists" means the same as "If God exists, then he exists."

Hence

(6)″ "God has actual existence" does not mean the same as *S*; so "God exists" does not mean the same as "If God exists, then he exists."

A second reply to the envisaged objection is this: Let us mean by "X has real actual existence" that the sentence "X has actual existence" is (a) true and (b) not equivalent in meaning to any ontologically sterile conditional sentence. And consider the following argument:

(1)‴ The concept of God is the concept of a supremely perfect being.

(2)‴ The concept of real actual existence is the concept of a perfection (relative to God).

(3)‴ The concept of God stands to the concept of real actual existence as the concept of a mountain stands to the concept of a valley, i.e., it is a conceptual truth that God has real actual existence.

So

(4)‴ God has real actual existence.

What this argument shows is that "God has actual existence" expresses the non-ontologically sterile (nonconditional) truth that "God exists" expresses a non-ontologically sterile (nonconditional) truth. Or, at any rate, the contemplated argument establishes this unless "God" analytically entails "a being which has real actual existence and is omnipotent, omniscient, and perfectly good," in which case "God has real actual existence" is equivalent in meaning to the ontologically sterile conditional sentence "If a being which has real actual existence (etc.) exists, then he has real actual existence." But now this criticism can be countered by (a) introducing the concept of X's having actual real actual existence—i.e., of X's being such that the sentence "X has real actual existence" (i) expresses a truth and (ii) is not equivalent in meaning to any ontologically sterile conditional sentence—and (b) pointing out that the concept of God stands to the concept of having actual real actual existence as the concept of a mountain stands to the concept of a valley. It follows from this that "God has real actual existence" expresses the non-ontologically sterile (nonconditional) truth that "God has actual existence" expresses the non-ontologically sterile (nonconditional) truth that "God exists" expresses a non-ontologically sterile (nonconditional) truth. And it would surely be preposterous to claim at this point that "God" analytically entails "a being who has actual real actual existence," so that "God has actual real actual existence" is equivalent in meaning to "If God exists, then he has actual real actual existence." And as the regress that we are started on progresses, analytic entailment claims of the envisaged sort would become more and more incredible, i.e., it would become more and more incredible that "God" has such an immensely bloated meaning.

Or would it? I am claiming that "God exists," "God has actual existence," "God has real actual existence," etc. all express conceptual truths. And this may give rise to the following argument: "Whenever it is a conceptual truth that Xs are Ys, this is because the term which stands for Xs analytically entails the term which stands for Ys (or vice versa). Thus, it is a conceptual truth that squares are four-sided figures only because 'squares' analytically entails 'four-sided figures'; it is a conceptual truth that bachelors are unmarried adult males only because 'bachelors' analytically entails 'unmarried adult males'; and so on. And, by parity of reasoning, it is a conceptual truth that God exists only if 'God' analytically entails 'existent being'; it is a conceptual truth that God has actual existence only if 'God' analytically entails 'a being who has actual existence'; and so on. But now if 'God' analytically entails 'existent being', then 'God exists' is indeed equivalent to 'If God exists, then he exists' (since it means the same as the vacuous sentence 'An existent [omnipotent, omniscient, and perfectly good] being exists'); and if 'God' analytically entails 'a being who has actual existence', then 'God has actual existence' is indeed equivalent to 'If God exists, then he has actual existence' (since it means the same as the vacuous sentence 'A being who has actual existence [etc.] has actual existence'); and so on."

The reply is simply that there are conceptual truths which are expressed by sentences in which the subject term does *not* analytically entail the predicate term. "Socrates is a non-number" is an example, as is "Mail boxes are nonconscious." Surely both of these sentences express necessary, but non-vacuous (i.e., conceptual), truths, but just as surely "Socrates" does not analytically entail "nonnumber" and "mail boxes" does not analytically entail "nonconscious." And, closer to home, "The number 9 exists" certainly appears to express a conceptual truth, even though it is highly implausible that "the number 9" analytically entails "exists." In short, my objector is overlooking the fact that some conceptual truths are *de re*, rather than *de dicto*, necessary.[5]

III

Consider the following parody of my interpretation of Descartes's argument:[6]

    a) Let "minor deity" = df "a being who has all perfections, but only a modest degree of perfections which vary in degree, like knowledge and power."

Then

    b) the concept of a minor deity is the concept of a being who has all perfections (etc.).

    c) The concept of existence is the concept of a perfection.

Hence

    d) the concept of existence stands to the concept of a minor deity as the concept of a square stands to the concept of a four-sided figure, i.e., it is a conceptual truth that a minor deity exists.

So

    e) a minor deity really exists.

If this argument is sound, then it can, of course, be used to establish the existence, not just of a single minor deity, but of an indefinitely large number of such beings. Hence, ontological modesty dictates that we find some flaw in it. And, if Descartes's proof is to stand, this cannot also be a flaw in that argument.

But in fact the envisaged criticism can be rebutted: The concept of God is such that it is a necessary truth that if God exists, then God is a radically unique being, in the sense that it is logically impossible for any other being even to come close to rivalling him with respect to the degree and number of his perfections. (This conditional expresses a conceptual truth about God, since it would turn out false under most substitutions of proper names, nouns, or definite descriptions for "God.") But the concept of a minor deity is such that it is a necessary truth that if minor deities exist, then they rival God with respect to the *number* of their perfections. It follows that, given that God exists, minor deities are logically impossible. Now it is better than not (from the point of view of reason) that logically impossible things do not exist. Moreover, it is better than not that God exists and is unrivalled with respect to the number of his perfections. So it is better than not that minor deities do not exist, and hence, it is false that existence is a perfection *relative to minor deities.* But the following argument is obviously fallacious:

a)′ The concept of a minor deity is the concept of a being who possesses all properties which are perfections *relative to a minor deity.*

b)′ The concept of existence is the concept of a perfection *relative to God.*

Hence

c) the concept of existence stands to the concept of a minor deity as the concept of a square stands to the concept of a four-sided figure, i.e., it is a conceptual truth that minor deities exist.

So

d) minor deities really exist.

Moreover, there is no analogous argument which shows that existence is not a perfection *relative to God* and, hence, undermines Descartes's proof in a similar fashion.

However, this is not quite an end of the matter. For my critic may want to respond to the contemplated refutation by redefining minor deities as beings which possess all properties which are perfections *relative to God*, but only a modest degree of knowledge, power, and goodness, and by setting out the following reformulated parody:

a) ′ The concept of a minor deity is the concept of a being who possesses all properties which are perfections relative to God (etc.).

b) ′ The concept of existence is the concept of a perfection relative to God.

Hence

c) the concept of existence stands to the concept of a minor deity as the concept of a square stands to the concept of a four-sided figure, i.e., it is a conceptual truth that minor deities exist.

So

d) minor deities really exist.

The reply to this latest parody is simply this: Since the concept of God is such that if God exists, then it is logically impossible for any other being to possess all of God's perfections, the present concept of a minor deity is, if God exists, logically incoherent. So if God exists, it is false that it is a conceptual truth that minor deities exist, since if God exists, then it is necessarily false that minor deities exist, and, needless to say, necessary falsehoods cannot be conceptual truths. (Again, premisses like a) ′ and b) ′ establish only a *prima facie* case for conclusions like c).) It follows that (given — what we have no reason to disbelieve at this point — that God exists) premiss c) of the latest parody is false, and, hence, that the parody is unsound. However, there is no similar argument which shows that the concept of God is logically incoherent; thus my refutation of the contemplated parody leaves Descartes's proof unscathed.

It is of note that the above refutation of the envisaged parodies also serves to refute the following argument: "Let 'major deity' = df 'a being who has the same number and degree of perfections that God possesses, except that he differs from God with respect, say, to the degree of love which he feels for us'. Then it can be shown that it is a conceptual truth that a major deity (and, indeed, an indefinitely large number of major deities) exist by an argument which closely parallels Descartes's proof." The reply is that the concept of God is, once again, such that it is a necessary truth that if God exists, then one of his major perfections is being unrivalled with respect to the number and degree of his perfections. It follows that any major deity would, if he existed, possess this perfection. And it follows in turn that given that a major deity exists, only that major deity is logically possible. Moreover, if we define "major deity" in such a way that *God* is a major deity, then the one logically possible major deity is God (given — what we have no reason to disbelieve at this point — that God exists). Hence, the concept of a major deity *other* than God is logically incoherent; so it is *not* a conceptual truth that such a being exists.

IV

William L. Rowe has offered the following criticism[7] of my defense of Descartes's Meditation V proof: "Let 'magican' = df 'an existing magician'. It follows from this definition that no nonexisting object is, or can be, a magican. For given this definition of 'magican', a nonexisting object can be a magican only if a nonexisting object can be an existing object, and that is plainly not the case. But now suppose — what is surely possible — that there never have been any magicians. Then no *existing* objects would be magicans either, and so magicans would be neither existing nor nonexisting objects.

"Now let us apply this to Dore's defense of Descartes's proof. Even if Dore has established that 'God exists' expresses a conceptual truth and, hence, does not mean the same as the vacuous sentence 'If God exists, then he exists', it does not follow that God really does exist. For it is open to us to construe 'God exists' as meaning 'No nonexisting object is God'. And just as it does not follow from the fact that no nonexisting object is a magican that magicans really do exist, so it does not follow from the fact that no nonexisting object is God that God really does exist. (However 'No nonexisting object is God' expresses a conceptual — rather than a vacuous — truth, since it would not continue to express a truth no matter what proper names, nouns, or definite descriptions we might substitute for 'God' in that sentence.)"

Now Rowe's criticism essentially involves the thesis that there are existing and nonexisting objects, and since nonexisting objects are notoriously controversial entities, it seems reasonable to try to make sure that talk about them — and their counterparts, existing objects — can be paraphrased into discourse which obeys the laws of logic. The most obvious suggestion for getting a logical handle on sentences of the form "X is a non-existing object" and sentences of the form "X is an existing object" is to require that the former sentence means (or, anyway, entails) "X does not exist" and that the latter sentence means (or, anyway, entails) "X does exist." Given that way of construing the former pair of sentences, they express contradictory propositions, from which it follows that if X is not a nonexisting object, then it is an existing object. But Rowe evidently does not construe them in the contemplated way, since he claims that, in the event that there were no magicians, magicans would be neither nonexisting objects nor existing objects.

Well, then, what is the logical status of objects which are neither existing objects nor nonexisting objects? What, on Rowe's view, is the logical status of magicans, given that there are no magicians? The answer is that they are logically impossible objects, since "the set of possible things can be exhaustively divided into those possible things which actually exist and those possible things which do not exist."[8] If Rowe is right, then things are either nonexisting objects or existing objects or logically impossible objects, some of which (like Rowe's magicans in the event that there are no magicians) are not also nonexisting objects.

Now it is surely a necessary truth that it is logically impossible for an object to be such that it neither exists nor does not exist. And Rowe is presumably trying to conform his view to that fact when he agrees that an object which is neither an existing object nor a nonexisting object is a logically impossible object, i.e., he is trying not to lose *all* logical control over objects which are neither existing nor nonexisting objects. Unfortunately, however, in agreeing that objects which are neither existing nor nonexisting objects are *ipso facto* logically impossible objects, he runs afoul of a necessary modal truth. Consider magicans again. If Rowe is right, then, given that there are no magicians, magicans are neither existing nor nonexisting objects and, hence, are logically impossible objects. But surely, even if there *are* no magicians, it is *logically possible* that there are magicians; and surely it is a necessary truth that if magicians exist, then they are magicans (existing magicians). It follows that, in maintaining that, given that there are no magicians, then magicans are logically impossible objects, Rowe is in effect denying the following necessary truth: When it is logically possible that something, X, (e.g., a magician or a square) exists, and it is also logically necessary that if it exists, then it is a Y (e.g., a magican or a four-sided figure), then it is logically possible that a Y exists.[9] (I am assuming here that sentences of the form "A Y is a logically impossible object" entail sentences of the form "It is logically impossible that a Y exists." Rowe can deny this entailment only if he provides us with much more information about the concept of a logically impossible object than in fact he has given us.)

But can we do any better? What *would* be the status of magicans in the event that there were no magicians? Suppose that we tried to get the concept of nonexisting objects under logical control by agreeing that sentences of the form "X is a nonexisting object" entail sentences of the form "X does not exist." And suppose we said that if there were no magicians, magicans would not exist. Would not that commit us to the unacceptable proposition that there would be at least one nonexisting object which is an existing object? But surely it would be just as unacceptable to maintain that magicans *would* exist, even if there were no magicians.

The question before us is "How can magicans be nonexisting objects?" Rowe presumably subscribes to the following argument that they cannot be:

a) It is a necessary truth that magicans are existing magicians.

b) It is a necessary truth that no nonexisting object is an existing magician.

So

c) it is a necessary truth that no magican is a nonexisting object.

But consider the following, analogous argument:

a)′ It is a necessary truth that dragons are fearsome animals with fiery breaths.

b)′ It is a necessary truth that no nonexisting object has the property of being a fearsome animal with a fiery breath.

Hence

c)′ it is a necessary truth that no dragon is a nonexisting object.

Presumably Rowe would not wish to maintain that this argument is sound. Surely any discourse about nonexisting objects, the rules of which forbid dragons (and, for an exactly similar reason, centaurs and so on indefinitely) to count among their number, is too logically disreputable to be worthy of serious consideration.

But what is *wrong* with the present argument? One answer is this: To say that dragons are nonexisting objects is not to ascribe the property of being a fearsome animal with a fiery breath to some nonexisting things. Rather it is to say that things *which are such that if they exist, then they are fearsome animals with fiery breaths* are nonexisting objects. This way of construing the former assertion has the advantage of allowing us to say that dragons are nonexisting objects, while making it unnecessary for us to agree that some nonexisting objects have the property (remarkable in nonexisting objects) of being fearsome animals with fiery breaths.

But then, by parity of reasoning, there is nothing to prevent us from maintaining that magicans would be nonexisting objects if there were no magicians. For in so doing we would be asserting, not that some nonexisting objects have the property of being existing objects, but rather that things *which are such that if they exist, then they are existing magicians* are nonexisting objects. And there is surely nothing logically wrong with that.

However, though this approach to the concepts of nonexisting dragons and nonexisting magicans saves us from logical absurdity, it entails that nonexisting objects do in fact have rather remarkable properties. Thus, though the present approach avoids the conclusion that some nonexisting objects have the property of being fearsome animals with fiery breaths, it commits us to the conclusion that some nonexisting objects have the dispositional property of being such that if they exist, then they are fearsome animals with fiery breaths. And, similarly, the present approach commits us to attributing to some nonexisting objects the dispositional property of being such that if they exist, then they are existing magicians. But the thesis that nonexisting objects can have such *dispositional* properties looks sufficiently implausible on its face that it is surely in need of defense.

One obvious move to make at this point is just to deny that, e.g., "Dragons do not exist" is best explicated by "Dragons are nonexisting objects." A very plausible alternative is that the former sentence is best taken to mean the same as "Nothing is a dragon." But then, by parity of reasoning, "Magicans do not exist" means "Nothing is a magican." And surely *that* translation does not support the thesis that magicans neither exist nor do not exist in the event that there are no magicans.

But it may be that there is another alternative open to us, namely, to adduce a defense of the claim that there are nonexisting objects which possess the envisaged dispositional properties. I have the following defense in mind: (1) Since possible-world semantics plays an important role in logical theory and is clearly a deep explication of our ordinary modal concepts, possible worlds are eminently ontologically respectable. (2) Possible, but not actual, individuals are as likely to exist (in merely possible worlds) as are possible, but not actual, worlds likely to exist. (3) Hence, the former provide an ontologically respectable subject for "has the dispositional property of being such that if it exists (in the actual world), then it is a dragon, an existing magician, etc." to be true of. (It seems likely that, e.g., a possible dragon is a possible *dragon*, as distinct from, e.g., a possible *unicorn* in virtue of the fact that if it existed in the actual world, then it would be a dragon, as opposed to a unicorn, there.)

But, to return to Rowe, if "Magicans are nonexisting objects" is best taken to mean "Magicans (existing magicians) are (merely) possible objects (though if they existed in the actual world, they would be actual magicians)," then since there is no temptation to think that this latter sentence expresses a logically inconsistent proposition, Rowe's defense of the thesis that there are objects which are neither existing nor nonexisting is a failure. It follows that there is no acceptable alternative to the claim that if "God exists" (1) expresses a truth and (2) is not equivalent in meaning to "If God exists, then he exists," then God, as Descartes says, really does exist.

Michael Scriven has criticized St. Anselm's version of the ontological argument as follows:

> the sense in which it is true that God "necessarily exists" is not a sense from which one can conclude that there has to be a God. The first claim is translatable as "Nothing can properly be called God

that does not really exist"; the second claim is "God really does exist"; and you cannot get either one from the other.[10]

But now can *anything* that does not really exist be properly called by *any* name? Scriven's argument would be pointless if the answer were No. So presumably Scriven would say that, e.g., "Superman" properly names a nonexisting object. If this is right, then Scriven is claiming in effect that (unlike Superman) God cannot be a nonexisting object, but that the latter proposition is compatible with God's not existing. Scriven's objection, then, amounts to the same thing as Rowe's and can be refuted in an exactly similar manner.

Finally, it should be noticed that my defense of Descartes's proof does not commit me to holding that magicans would not be nonexisting objects even if there were no magicians. An ontological argument for the existence of magicans would have exactly the same dubious status as the section II "proof" of the existence of existent winged horses. For just as "existent" operates as a logical particle in "Existent winged horses exist," so that the sentence expresses a vacuous, rather than a conceptual, truth, so, too, "existing" operates as a logical particle in "Magicans (i.e., existing magicians) exist," so that *that* sentence expresses a vacuous, rather than a conceptual, truth, i.e., even though it expresses a necessary truth, it does not entail that magicans really do exist.

NOTES

1. René Descartes, *The Philosophical Works of Descartes*, trans. Haldane and Ross, vol. 1 (New York: Dover Publications, 1955), p. 181.

2. Anthony Kenny points out that Descartes explained to a critic that by "a mountain without a valley" he meant an uphill slope without a downhill slope. Anthony Kenny, *Descartes, A Study of His Philosophy* (New York: Random House, 1968), p. 156.

3. When *any* sentence expresses a truth, this is at least *in part* explicable by reference to the concepts which it expresses.

4. Descartes claims that the idea of God—like the idea of geometrical figures—is not *made* by the mind, but rather *discovered* to be part of its contents. He says of his idea of God: "I discern . . .

that this idea is not something factitious, and depending solely on my thought." Haldane and Ross, *Philosophical Works of Descartes*, vol. 1, p. 182). And he says of his idea of a certain fiction—namely, a winged horse—which he has invented, that "just as I may imagine a winged horse, although no horse with wings exists, so I could perhaps attribute existence to God, although no God existed. But a sophism is concealed in this objection. . . . For it is not within my power to think of God without existence . . . though it is in my power to imagine a horse either with wings or without wings." (Ibid., pp. 181-82) Here it appears that Descartes believes that there are no necessary truths about fictitious beings. But this is a mistake. Though winged horses are fictitious, the sentence "Winged horses are winged" surely expresses a necessary truth, as does "Existent winged horses exist." Still—as the above will make plain—Descartes need not have worried about such Gaunilo-type entities.

5. For a powerful defense of the doctrine of *de re* necessity, see Alvin Plantinga, *The Nature of Necessity* (London: Oxford University Press, 1974).

6. I am indebted to William L. Rowe for pointing this parody out to me.

7. At the 1981 Notre Dame Conference on the Philosophy of Religion on which this book is based. In formulating the objection I have drawn on Rowe's critique of Anselm's Proslogion II proof in William L. Rowe, *Philosophy of Religion: An Introduction* (Belmont, California: Dickenson, 1978), pp. 41-46.

8. Ibid., p. 43.

9. Paul Hamilton has called my attention to another objection to Rowe: If there are magicians, then *eo ipso* there are existing magicians, and, hence, magicans exist. But if magicans exist, then they are logically possible. But if Rowe is right, in possible worlds in which there are no magicians, magicans are logically impossible. So there are some possible worlds (e.g., the actual world) in which magicans are logically possible and some in which they are not. Hence, Rowe's argument entails the denial of the intuitive (S5) thesis that what is logically possible is necessarily logically possible.

10. Michael Scriven, *Primary Philosophy* (New York: McGraw-Hill, 1966), pp. 146-47.

The Names of God
and the Being of Names

MARK D. JORDAN

It is characteristic of the medieval Latins that they prefaced their discourses about the most intelligible being—about God—with assertions that such discourses would always fail to make the signified present. In these assertions of the *absence* of the highest signified, they thought not only to be obeying the precepts of Scripture but also to be agreeing with certain arguments in their ancient philosophic "authorities." These arguments showed the necessary failure of human signs with regard to the final signified.

I would like to trace such arguments in Aquinas, who figures decisively in the constitution of the doctrine of divine names. His teaching about them is not only a useful antidote to philosophic vanity; it is also a reflection on the fixed limit of linguistic intelligibility. That limit, I will suggest, is the nearest approach in philosophy to the nature of God. If one could see why human names fail to name God, then one would understand as much of the divine nature as can be *known* outside beatitude. One would also see, not coincidentally, that the signification of human signs rests on a signified which eludes them. The failure of discourse about God, on Thomas's account, lays bare the structure of language in a privileged disclosure. Such disclosure is the trace of the nature of God in human thinking. To say it bluntly: the surest approach to the divine is by the scrutiny of linguistic failure.

This paper will trace these possibilities only in the most preliminary way.[1] Its first section will offer a reading of one of

Aquinas's many passages on the divine names. The second section will trace the passage back into the *auctoritates* upon which Aquinas builds it. The third section will take the passage in its given context with an eye for the connection between the doctrine of the divine names and the philosophic conviction of God's simplicity. Finally, the fourth section will argue that the fact of such simplicity beyond language is required even in the failure of human language to speak it. In restoring the original order of the names of God and the being of names, one will gain a sounder philosophic access to the question of God's nature than can be provided by views of language which want an easy presence and literal intelligibility.[2]

Let me forestall one misunderstanding from the beginning. In what follows I will be treating the question of the divine names without investigating the details of the doctrine of analogy. If this should seem odd, it may be because there is frequently an identification of the doctrines of analogy and of the names in discussing Aquinas. While it is clear that the divine names are one instance of names said analogously, it is not the case that the study of analogy is the same as the study of the divine names.[3] The failure of human language with regard to God is a question to which a model for analogy provides only a partial answer. I am now interested in tracing the philosophic features of the question itself.

I. Aquinas on the Divine Names

The middle articles of the seventh question anthologized under the title *De potentia* are not the preferred locus in Thomas for the doctrine of the divine names. The seventh question is not explicitly devoted to the doctrine. When the question does treat of the names, it considers them parenthetically within the investigation of simplicity. Yet this treatment, however much it might seem indirect, has the advantages of the disputed questions generally as against the pedagogically constrained treatments of the so-called *Summa contra gentiles* or the *Prima pars* of the *Summa theologiae*. The disputed questions provide fully technical responses to advanced questions, without the elisions and simplifications required in teaching beginners. Their heuristic schemata tend to be more nuanced, and they are franker about their sources. There can be no chronological objection in this case, since the questions were disputed within a year of the composition of the parallel text in the last *Summa.*[4] For these exegetical reasons, as well as for the explicit connection with divine simplicity, I take as my text the central articles from *De potentia*, question 7.[5] My reading will follow the text rather closely, in order to avoid the vertigo of those who interpret philosophical positions in midair.

The movement from the consideration of divine simplicity to the consideration of its consequences for the divine names falls in the third article. The first two articles had asked whether God is simple and whether there is in him a distinction between *essentia* and *esse*. The third article now asks whether God falls into any of the genera. 'Genus' is, of course, a term which issues from the logical doctrine of definition; to ask whether God can be placed in a genus is already to broach the question of how he can be named. Aquinas gives three arguments in support of the claim that God is not in any genus. The first argument holds that nothing can be assigned to a genus according to its *esse*, but only according to its *ratio quidditatis* (*De pot.*, q. 7, a.3, c, 193:2).[6] Since God is his very *esse*, he cannot be assigned to any genus. The implication that God does not have a *ratio quidditatis* is clear and serves to reinforce the lesson already given in article 2 about the complete absence of composition in God.

The second argument against God's being in a genus depends again on the ground for assignment to a genus. Aquinas reasons that "however much matter is not genus, or form difference, nonetheless the *ratio generis* is taken from matter, and the *ratio differentiae* is taken from form" (q. 7, a.3, c, 193:2). Since there is in God nothing which could be likened to matter — neither matter itself nor any potency — it follows that genus cannot be applied to God. This second argument also depends on the lack of a composition in God of actuality and potentiality, a tenet already argued in the first article. The third argument reasons that God cannot be in any genus because a genus implies a finite determination to particular attributes (q. 7, a.3, c, 193:2-194:1). The characteristic of any genus is limitation within the field of possible genera, a limitation with regard to alternate perfections. God, however much marked off from creatures, is not limited by such exclusion.

The result of these arguments is to move Aquinas's thinking into the territory of the divine names. So the fourth article asks whether names like "good, wise, and just" are predicated of God accidentally. This is the ancient question about whether the divine attributes are accidents of the divine substance. Aquinas's answer is that they are not. His first argument asserts that there can be no accidental features in God because there is no difference in him between essence and substance or between participating and participated (q. 7, a.4, c, 195:2). There is no foothold in God for either material or intellectual accidents. Aquinas's second argument reasons that any accidental attribute, falling as it does outside the essence, must arise from the activity of some cause. But God is not subject to any cause (q. 7, a.4, c, 195:2-196:1). His third argument is that God cannot receive any accident because he has no potency. Names like 'good', 'wise', and 'just' are not, therefore, predicated of God accidentally.

I said that this was the ancient question about the divine attributes, and I will come back to its genealogy in the next section. But it is worth seeing now that Aquinas puts the issue in its strong form at once by taking attributes which seem pure. It is not a question of the gross anthropomorphisms — God as angry or as a lion or as a rock. Nor is it the question of God's intervention in history, his providential will. Thomas takes the pure case of the application of *likely* predicates to God. To that case he replies that the predicates cannot be construed as names of properties "in" God.

The positive side of the answer is, of course, that such names, if they are to name at all, must name something about God which is not accidental. How can this be? In the reply to the first objection Aquinas recalls a favorite distinction, the distinction between *what* a word predicates (*id quod predicat*) and that *from which* the word is taken (*id a quo imponitur ad significandum*; q. 7, a. 4, ad 1m, 196:1). Although the distinction has several applications in Aquinas,[7] it is here the distinction between the word's referent and its genesis, between its final cause and its efficient one. All human words arise from the signification of accidental forms which we find in bodies or the embodied. The names of God are projected beyond this origin to signify something nonaccidental in the incorporeal. That projection removes the use of a word from its ordinary logical contexts as well as from its ordinary meaning. However much the word 'good' falls in its ordinary use within the category of quality, it is lifted out of that category when used of God.

If the divine names are not said accidentally, are they then said of God substantially? By way of an answer Aquinas returns in the fifth article to the starting point of his treatment of the divine names. He sketches two responses, the first more radical than the second, to the question whether the names name at all. These two seem to Aquinas the only responses worth long consideration. The first is that of Maimonides; the second, that of Pseudo-Dionysius. On Aquinas's reading, Maimonides holds that no divine name signifies the divine substance. Either such names signify by likeness to effects, or they signify in the way of negation. To take a signification of the first sort: God is called "wise," says Maimonides, because his effects seem to men to show wise action. To take a signification of the second sort: God is called "living" in order to stress that he is not inanimate. The two explanations are not mutually exclusive; both names seem susceptible of both sorts of explanation.

Aquinas rejects Maimonides's radical proposal that the divine names do not name anything about God. He argues against Maimonides's first model — that of analogy to the effects — by saying that this would put names such as 'wrathful' and 'fiery' on the same footing with names such as 'wisdom', since God's effects certainly seem at times like wrath and like fire. Moreover, Aquinas argues, Maimonides's first form of signification would make meaningful predication about God dependent on the existence of his effects, thus denying the intelligible articulation of divine features in the absence of creatures (q.7, a.5, c, 198:1).

Aquinas rejects Maimonides's second model for signification on the grounds that every name involves some negation in its being distinct from other names. Thus God can be called "lion" in order to stress that he is not a bird, and also "bird," since he is not a lion. More fundamentally, Aquinas holds that every act of negation depends upon the prior grasp of an affirmation. Maimonides would deny such a prior grasp in favor of pure negativity and would thus rob the language of meaning (q.7, a.5, c, 198:1-2).

The rejection of the Maimonidean models takes the form of an argument from the practice of speaking about God. Aquinas seems to be assuming that there is a hierarchy of meaningful predications about God—and so rejects the first model as destructive of the order of the hierarchy. He seems to assume that some things are legitimately said of God while others are not—and so rejects the second Maimonidean model as destructive of distinction in what is said. For both cases Aquinas seems to hold that all things said of God are not equal. Is this a defensible assumption? I want to hold off a semantic answer to that question for a moment. Still, it is worth pointing out that the assumption is in no way theological. The examples which Aquinas uses to illustrate the *illegitimate* ways of speaking are more nearly theological and scriptural than the examples he uses for the legitimate predications. God is wrathful, fiery, is a lion and a bird. These are for Aquinas predications taken from among the lower of the divine names. They are also taken from the language of the Scriptures. It is not true, then, that Aquinas is assuming the privileged place of the scriptural speech about God. On the contrary, Aquinas relies on a philosophic practice within which 'good', 'wise', 'just', and other such terms become the privileged predications.

Having set aside the radical alternative of Maimonides, Aquinas turns to the more moderate proposal, as he construes it, of Pseudo-Dionysius. On this proposal the divine names do signify the divine substance; they do name, but imperfectly. Aquinas explains the manner of predication by comparing it to the relations of likeness which obtain between cause and effect. The comparison is not arbitrary. Causal likeness is for Thomas the privileged relation of likeness because the least arbitrary. *Every* cause causes its like.[8] Likeness is not something added to causality; it is of the very nature of causality as activity (*pace* Lonergan).[9] Since creatures are effects of God's causal activity, the likeness of creatures to God is the securest ground for the divine names.[10]

So Thomas distinguishes, as he customarily does, between adequate and inadequate effects (q. 7, a. 5, c, 198:2). Since no effect is adequate to God's full activity, creatures represent a splintering of the attributes which are united in God. Human intellects become like the creatures that they understand. They become like the splintered likenesses of God. This allows an imperfect speech about the divine substance to be constructed on the basis of human understanding. It is imperfect, not in the way that an incomplete induction is imperfect, but in the way that a textbook reproduction of a master's painting is imperfect. However useful the reproduction might be, one must be reminded daily of its limitations. In the case of God, where no adequate imitation is possible in principle, the reminder becomes paramount. So Thomas adds that one can see why the name that God gave to Moses, the name '*Qui est*', is the best of the divine names.[11] It specifies no form, it sets no limits, but simply calls God by what is, in a way, the most common name. The name '*Qui est*', Thomas recalls from John Damascene, signifies an "infinite sea of substance" ("*substantiae pelagus infinitum*," q. 7, a. 5, c, 199:1).[12]

The refracted signification of the divine names is stated more technically in the reply to an objection (q. 7, a. 5, ad 2m, 199:2). The divine names are to be said of God with regard to what they signify, but not with regard to *how* they signify. Their mode of signification is to say anything as if it were a finite attribute. Yet the things which are named by such constricted names are imperfect likenesses of "things" which are in God nonattributively. So it is that one gets the three-step dialectic of Pseudo-Dionysius. One first affirms the names of God with the understanding that there is something *like* goodness or justice in God. But one then has to negate the names, second, since what is in God is not like what human language means by such terms. In the third step one negates the mode of signification implicit in the names while affirming what they intend to signify. One begins, that is, to predicate the names of God "supereminently" (q. 7, a. 5, ad 2m, 199:2; cf. ad 5m).

Even if we can negate the mode of signification while retaining its intention, it does not follow that we can think the simplicity of God — this is the burden of the sixth article. The divine names do not become synonyms from our point of view, even though they refer to what is absolutely simple.[13] Thomas argues the point in two parts. The first states, rather simply, that the divine names are not synonymous because they preserve different intentional perspectives on the one, simple divinity. Thomas here rehearses his basic lesson in semantics: words do not refer to things except by means of understanding (q. 7, a. 6, c, 201:1-2). Thomas sees that this statement requires a second remark. If the names refer to something absolutely simple under various intentional perspectives, why is the diversity of the names anything more than a lie? What ground could a diversity of perspectives have in the simplicity of God?

Thomas can answer such doubts only by providing a schema by which to classify the various ways in which ideas correspond to the things of the world. In the first case which Thomas considers there *is* no correspondence. This case is the class of terms such as 'genus' and 'species' which are second intentions derived by the reflection of the mind on its own modes of understanding. The notional distinctions preserved in the divine names do not belong to this first class, since the divine names are not about how God is understood. That was the force of the argument against Maimonides, to show that the divine names are not second intentions. The next case Aquinas considers is the class of terms which correspond to the diversity of effects due to the thing named (q. 7, a. 6, c, 201:2–202:1). But such terms require that one understand the cause before its effects. If we say "Mozart is witty" and also "Mozart is a master of melody," it is because we already know that Mozart is the maker of both the *Musical Joke* and also of the *Magic Flute*. Prior knowledge of divine causality is not possible for us. Moreover, such an argument would allow that God could be called by the name of anything which he had created, and so 'sky' or 'snake' would become divine names. There would also follow, again, the (hypothetical) difficulty of naming God before creation.

It must be, Thomas concludes, that the notional differences in the divine names correspond in some third way to a ground in the divine nature. This is the way in which many partial images can be made of one original (q. 7, a. 6, c, 202:1). The plurality of the names is due to the inability of any created intellect to make a single adequate image of God. The true vision of God — just as the true Word of God — abolishes plurality. But to see as much is grace, not the philosophic doctrine of the divine names.

It remains for Thomas to write in the seventh article a coda to these various movements. When asked whether the divine names are said univocally or equivocally of God and his creatures, Thomas replies that neither is the case. The names are not said univocally because no creature is an adequate effect of the divine power; its mode of existing is too diminished to allow of univocity (q. 7, a. 7, c, 203:2-204:1). The names are not pure equivocity, as Maimonides held, since they exhibit a hierarchical, participational order. So it is that Thomas arrives at the analogy of the divine names. He distinguishes analogy here into an analogy of two things in virtue of a third, and an analogy of two things, one in respect of the other. Since there is no third thing beyond God and creatures, the analogy of the divine names is an analogy of the second type (q. 7, a. 7, c, 204:1). Notice that the doctrine of analogy makes its appearance at the conclusion of the treatment of the names, after one has wrestled with the question of whether they name at all. The same is true of Aquinas's other treatments.[14] The disproportionate fascination which since Cajetan the classification of analogy has exercised on Thomas's readers obscures the features of the names themselves. Those features become questionable in Thomas's predecessors under the rubric of the consideration of the divine attributes.

II. The *Auctoritates* and the Divine Names

One would expect, from the emphasis on analogy, that Aristotle would appear as the chief *auctoritas* for the construction of the doctrine of the divine names in Aquinas. In fact, the sequence of articles from *De potentia* uses two other *auctoritates* as the main interlocutors: Pseudo-Dionysius and Maimonides. Behind Pseudo-Dionysius — as behind the citations to John Damascene — stand the Neo-Platonic writers, whose doctrine of the ineffability of the divine goes back through Plotinus and Albinus to the construal of the first "thesis" of Plato's *Parmenides*.[15] Behind Maimonides stand the apophatic traditions in Judaism and Islam.[16] Thomas works out his position on the divine names in the middle of these authorities; he thinks with them. The alternatives represented by Pseudo-Dionysius and Maimonides become for Thomas the boundaries of fruitful debate about the names. It is necessary, then, to place his teaching in the conversation of the *auctoritates*. The Maimonidean alternative will receive much shorter treatment because it occupies a much smaller space in Aquinas's writings.

In Aquinas's own exposition of the whole text of the *Divine Names*, he places that work within what he takes to be the hierarchy of the Dionysian corpus. He divides "*artificialiter*" into four steps "those things about God which are contained in the Sacred Scriptures" (*In div. nom.*, prooemium, n. 1).[17] There are, first, those things which "pertain to the unity of the divine essence and the distinction of persons," matters beyond any natural analogue; such names are expounded in the *Divine Hypotyposes*.[18] Names which are said of God by means of natural analogues are next divided into two kinds. There are appellations which descend from God to creatures, such as goodness or life; these are treated in the work at hand, the *Divine Names*. Then there are names which are translated from creatures to God, such as 'lion', 'rock', 'sun'. These metaphorical names are treated by Pseudo-Dionysius in the *Symbolic Theology*. Finally, there comes the recognition of the radical deficiency of all creatures with regard to God, who remains still "*occultum et ignotum*." This recognition Pseudo-Dionysius treats in his fourth work, the *Mystical Theology*. Thomas finds that the works of the Dionysian corpus correspond to the four different types of divine names in Scripture.

Pseudo-Dionysius begins the *Divine Names* itself by limiting what can be spoken of God to those names handed on by Scripture. Thomas adds this justification: "This is also observed in the human sciences, that starting-points (*principia*) and conclusions are from the same genus. So therefore the starting-points from which this teaching (*doctrina*) proceeds are those which are received from the Holy Spirit by revelation and had in the Sacred Scriptures" (c. 1, lect. 1, §11, 7:1). This is an Aristotelian maxim introduced in support of a scriptural claim. Pseudo-Dionysius continues: God is inaccessible in himself but becomes mediately accessible in many illuminations and manifestations which are received according to the various powers of the created receivers. Thomas adds to these principles an explanation of the exact sense in which any creature can only reach up to God through created similitudes (c. 1, lect. 1, §§29-30). It is from creatures, Thomas reiterates, that human names are drawn. They are legitimately drawn from creatures insofar as the divine goodness has illuminated them to some extent. But such illuminations are received only by holy minds, whose capacity is determined by divine concession and by their own conditions (c. 1, lect. 1, §§38-39).

Pseudo-Dionysius next describes our access to the divine through praise in response to the transforming call of God. The call comes in "symbolic" form. To read scriptural speech is to pass through the multiplicity of "vestments" to the divine simplicity from which they derive. Thomas adds that the form of such communication is due to God's benignity: "(The fact) that in the Scriptures intelligible things are expressed to us by sensibles, and supersubstantial things by existents (*existentia*), and incorporeals by corporeals, and simple things by the composite and diverse, is not on account of envy, so that the knowing of divine things might be taken away from us, but for our utility, since the Scripture, condescending to us, gives us those things which are above us according to our mode. And this very mode of knowing is how we can come to know God in the present life" (c. 1, lect. 2, §65, 20:2).

How is the condescension of scriptural language to be accepted? There seem to be two sides to Pseudo-Dionysius's answer. On the one hand, he remarks that many holy minds, having experienced union with God, will speak nothing but negations of the divine. On the other hand, the Holy Scriptures use many names of God, some of them drawn from participated attributes, others from homelier things. The plurality of names is justified in view of God's comprehending everything that is.

Thomas makes these two sides of Pseudo-Dionysius's answer into a simple progression. "For this is the last thing to which we can attain regarding the divine knowledge in this life, that God is above everything that can be thought by us, and so the naming (*nominatio*) of God which is by remotion is most proper" (c. 1, lect. 3, §83, 28:1). But there is a second way of naming God, which approaches him "as cause." The likeness of cause and effect, which is not extrinsic but essential, allows one to name God from his effects, however mediately. Thomas insists, against the *Platonici*, that all such effects fall out from the one cause (c. 1, lect. 3, §100). God's universal rule is not only the best government, but it is also the universal ground upon which the names can stand as expressing causal likenesses (c. 1, lect. 3, §99). With that doctrine Pseudo-Dionysius turns to consider the "intelligible" names of God, beginning with the divine unity in trinity.

There are obvious differences between Aquinas's exposition of Pseudo-Dionysius and his own teaching in the articles from *De potentia*. The exposition follows Pseudo-Dionysius in restricting the names to those with scriptural authority, while the articles seemed to move rather in the realm of philosophic discourse. The doctrine of God's mediate manifestation is treated in the exposition always theologically and Christocentrically, while the same doctrine is stated more neutrally in *De potentia* as a principle of causation. In these and other instances the exegete's work with regard to the exposition is to discern how Aquinas transforms Pseudo-Dionysius in commenting upon him.[19] But I must set that question aside, together with the examination of the differences between the exposition and the articles, in order to underscore what remains the same — that permanent doctrine which Aquinas learns from Pseudo-Dionysius.

In a suggestive, if violent, reading of Pseudo-Dionysius, Jean-Luc Manion argues that the task of the divine names is to find a language capable of speaking the distance which separates human knowing from God.[20] A language which cannot mark that distance, or which tries to abolish it, is idolatrous. One must resist, then, both the presumption of a language which seeks to become identical with its referents and the presumption of a language which closes in on itself as its own referent. In either case the language would claim to exhaust its objects in predication.[21] One resists these presumptions by the ways of eminence and negation, which are not additional categories of predication so much as gestures which seek to point beyond such categories altogether.[22] It becomes possible to point beyond in part because God himself gives a name — gives many names — which are marks of his otherness, of his transcendent anteriority.[23] It is especially possible to point beyond in the language of praise, by which the hierarchical reception and return to the divine gift are accomplished.[24] Hymns do not predicate but rather treat the divine as the inexpressible source of the gifts which are hierarchically received. The distance marked by the divine names is a distance which is overcome in the language of praise.

I said that Manion's reading was suggestive and violent.[25] While I do not think that the reading could be applied in all its details to the Dionysian texts, or that Aquinas would find it completely acceptable as an exposition, I do think that the notion of the divine names as names which invoke God while marking the distance which separates us from him can be found in Aquinas precisely as the doctrine of negation or remotion. Let me illustrate this with two passages from the exposition of the *Divine Names*.

The first illustrative passage comes from the remarks on the seventh chapter, in which Pseudo-Dionysius considers the names 'sapientia', 'mens', and so on (c. 7, lect. 1-5). The exposition of the whole chapter is very rich for the doctrine of negation. But the most striking remarks on negation come from the *lectio* in which Aquinas comments on the points which Pseudo-Dionysius makes about the manner in which God is known (c. 7, lect. 4). What Thomas offers here, beyond the teaching of the articles from *De potentia*, is a triple scheme of ascent to God by means of likeness, which is found either by remotion ("in omnium ablatione")[26] or by excess or by causality. The conclusion which follows upon the study of these three ways is that human knowing is inverted as it approaches the divine. Aquinas states it paradoxically: "Even on account of this is God known by our knowing, since whatever falls into our knowing, we accept as brought from him, and again [he] is known by our ignorance, namely, inasmuch as this is to know God, that we know that we do not know of God what he is" (c. 7, lect. 4, §731, 274:1). Similar paradoxical couplets follow: God is known and not, is named and not, is sensed and not. These are resolved in that union with God which exceeds them in the perfection of remotion. The soul learns that "God is not only above all things which are below it, but even above it itself and above all things which can be comprehended by it. And thus knowing God, in such a state of knowing, it is illuminated by that depth of divine Wisdom, which we cannot investigate (*perscrutari*)" (c. 7, lect. 4, §732, 275:2).

The same point is made more forcefully in the second passage which I extract to illustrate the place of negation. The passage comes from the penultimate *lectio* of Thomas's commentary and concerns the teaching of divine unity in Pseudo-Dionysius's final pages, just before the epilogue. Pseudo-Dionysius is considering the only proper way in which unity, the final attribute, is said of God. Thomas concludes: "And since the theologians judge that every name we impose falls short of God, therefore 'they' put first among all the modes by which we can ascend to God through intellect, that which is 'by negations', by which we ascend to God in a certain order" (c. 13, lect. 3, §995, 369:2). Negation is the means of ascent: "our soul by negating proceeds 'through all the divine understandings', " "our soul is joined to God, in ascending by negations'," (c. 13, lect. 3, §996, 370:1). It is negation which marks the epistemological limit of the present life. "And a certain joining of the soul with God is had in as much as it is possible to be joined to God now: our intellect is not at present joined to God so as to see his essence, but so as to know of God what He is not" (c.13, lect. 3, §996, 370:2).

How is this negation, which Aquinas seems to approve in the exposition of Pseudo-Dionysius, different from the position of Maimonides, which he elsewhere rejects? Let me qualify this question before addressing it. The exegetical difficulties of Maimonides's *Guide for the Perplexed* are as great as those of any other text known to me, not excluding the Scriptures, of which Maimonides may be providing an imitation in the philosophic order. Leo Strauss has argued convincingly that the unraveling of the *Guide*'s deliberate esotericism requires a meticulous balancing of contradictory statements and implications drawn from different parts of the work.[27] I will take the question about Maimonides, then, as a question about Maimonides as he was read by Aquinas.

The reconciliation of the multiple predications of attributes with divine simplicity occurs in the first book of the *Guide*, in which a general treatment (chapters 50-60) is followed by a review of the traditional names of God, including the tetragrammaton (chapters 61-64). These chapters seem to lie behind the references to Maimonides which occur in various of Aquinas's treatments of the divine names.[28] For example, Aquinas writes that Maimonides construed the names of God as names of remotion: "Some say that all of these names, even if they are said affirmatively of God, are nonetheless found rather to be taking something away from God, than to be positing something in him. . . . And this was put forward by Rabbi Moses" (1 *ST*, q. 13, a. 2, c). The example used is the assertion that God is "living." That example is taken from Maimonides's *Guide*: "Of this thing we say that it exists, the meaning being that its nonexistence is impossible. We apprehend further that this being is not like the being of the elements, for example, which are dead bodies. We say accordingly that this being is living, the meaning being that He, may He be exalted, is not dead."[29] Maimonides adds, after a list of similar glosses on other attributive predications: "It has thus become clear to you that every attribute that we predicate of Him is an attribute of action or, if the attribute is intended for the apprehension of His essence and not of His action, it signifies the negation or the privation of the attribute in question."[30]

What distinguishes this form of negation from the Dionysian? The Maimonidean negation is a logical qualification which is put on words even as they are used; the qualification is so severe that it renders them logically equal. The Dionysian negation is an epistemological reversal which is applied to predicates as the mind moves through them into union with God. The reason that the Maimonidean negation must be rejected is that without some predications one cannot begin the passage to God. The Dionysian negation, coming as it does in the end, allows one something with which to begin the ascent.

Now I do not think that this criticism affects Maimonides directly, since the pedagogical intentions of the *Guide* are rather different from what Thomas seems to imagine.[31] But I do think that the rejection of Maimonides by Aquinas is a rejection of an explanation which would vitiate hierarchical ascent, which would suppress the distance between God and creature by turning away from it. For that reason, precisely to preserve the hierarchical tension of the names, Aquinas refuses to follow Maimonides's dichotomy of names as a general rule.[32] There is one case, however, in which Aquinas agrees with Maimonides in taking what is apparently a positive name and reading it negatively from the start. Indeed, this is not only the final negation: it is also the first negation. It is the beginning of the doctrine of the names altogether. I mean the name 'one', which is the name of divine simplicity.

III. The Simplicity of the Divine Essence

The connection between the question of the divine names and the assertion that the divine essence is absolutely simple comes not only in Thomas's *auctoritates* but in the context of his arguments about the divine names in *De potentia*. There the divine names are treated parenthetically within a consideration of the simplicity of the divine essence and the subsequent reinterpretation of relations to God. The arguments presented in both sections are similar to arguments which Aquinas advances in many other texts.[33] They are not the delimitation of another attribute; they are the discovery of the very problem about attributes.[34]

There are three reasons, Thomas writes in the first article, for holding that God is "simple in every way" ("*simplicem modis omnibus*," *De pot.* q. 7, a. 1, c, 189:1). The first relies on the previously established hierarchy of entities. All entities have been shown to proceed from one completely actual entity, which is entirely lacking in potency. But every composition implies some potency, either of one part to another or of all parts to the whole. Lacking such potency, there is no receptivity for composition. God, being wholly actual, cannot be a composite.

The second reason why God cannot be composite lies in the genesis of any composition. In a compound the various elements must be brought together by something; there must be some prior agent responsible for bringing about the composition. Since no agent is prior to God, he cannot be composite (q. 7, a. 1, c, 189:1).

The third reason has to do with notions of perfection. God is the perfect being who lacks nothing. But every compound is imperfect and lacks something. The good of the composition is precisely in its being compounded; the good of the whole is not actually in any of the parts. The parts lack it and so do not have the highest sort of perfection. It follows, for a third time, that God cannot be a composite (q. 7, a. 1, c, 189:1-2).

The objections *against* the claim of simplicity are something like a catalogue of the problems with divine transcendence from the philosophy of antiquity. If God is simple, how can he make a world of multiplicity? If God is simple, how can he exhibit a distinction between essence and properties? The most pertinent of the objections are those which touch directly on the multiple predications made of God. The fifth objector, for example, argues that since it is possible to affirm truly a communicability of essence while denying truly a communicability of property, God must be multiple (q. 7, a. 1, obj. 5, 188:2). Thomas replies that there is nothing impermissible about contrary predications in cases where one thing is understood under several different *"rationes,"* different notions. The same point on a line may, in a geometrical demonstration, be treated as the end of one segment and the beginning of another (q. 7, a. 1, ad 5m, 189:2). A similar answer is given to the broad objection that various predicates cannot be applied to God.

The second article of the seventh question asks whether *substantia* or *essentia* are identified in God with *esse*. I will not enter into this famous discussion except to note that objections from true predication are again made (q. 7, a. 2, obj. 2, 7, 11). Thomas answers again with the familiar distinction between what is in the thing and what is in our way of understanding it or speaking about it (q. 7, a. 2, ad 2m, ad 7m, and especially ad 11m).

I would like to point out here too that the accounts are not theological in any strict sense. Thomas cites only three *auctoritates* in the body of the first article: Aristotle twice and Hilary from the *De trinitate* once. But one of the citations to Aristotle and the reference to Hilary are offered more as illustrations than as premises. The remaining citation to Aristotle is used in support of the philosophic claim that quasi-material potency is necessary for composition (q. 7, a. 1, c, 189:1, where the reference is to the *Physics*). It also seems important to note that there is no appeal to mystical vision or other direct experience of God, sources which are sometimes imputed to Plotinus as his justification for asserting the simplicity of the One.[35] The only mention of the contemplation of God in the first article is made by the second objector and deflected by Thomas (q. 7, a. 1, obj. 2 and ad 2m).

Indeed, the text of the first article shows plainly that Thomas derives the doctrine of simplicity not from theology but from the chief conclusions of his ontology. The simplicity of God is required by the place of God as the highest member — and thus the source — of the most comprehensive hierarchy. This position is seen in three ways: as an eminence of actuality, as an absolute priority in action, and as a perfection with regard to all qualities. The doctrine of the divine simplicity is a tenet from the inquiry of metaphysics and not from the revelation of Scriptures. It is then not the case, in Thomas's mind, that the problem of the divine names arises from anthropormorphic locutions in Scripture which must be excused. It is rather that metaphysical inquiry itself gives rise to the problem and to the doctrine. Even standing in the middle of the hierarchy, human language finds itself faced with the necessity of positing a being at the hierarchy's top in whom an absolute simplicity will save predication by undoing it.

I do not imagine that I have given even the beginning of a defense of the metaphysical discourse which underlies these claims. I have only wanted to show that the question of divine simplicity is treated by Thomas, in fact and in intention, as a question arising for metaphysics. This can be seen in the parallel passages as well. In both the *Summa contra gentiles* and the *Summa theologiae* the argument takes a different form. Thomas moves by remotion to argue against the attribution of a number of compositions to God, arriving in the end at the perfection of simplicity.[36] But in both of these other treatments the question of divine composition is treated immediately after the question of God's existence as one of the preparatory topics.

Granted that Thomas considered the matter metaphysical rather than theological, that he considered it preparatory rather than sophisticated, what is the justification for his treatment? There are several objections to it which can be set aside as inadequate; their failure will suggest, perhaps, some of the strengths in Thomas's position. The first objection would hold that the simplicity of God is argued upon the grounds of an outdated physics and of "Hellenistic" notions that identify perfection with what is uniquely apart. But the first half of this objection mistakes Thomas's language, which, even in its analysis of concrete beings, always recognizes that its general terms are second intentions, modally distinct from the instances which fall under them. Thomas is no easy believer in physical "results." The second half of the objection does not see that because of such self-correction and such tenacity over method, Thomas cannot be accused simply of metaphysical nostalgia or Eleatic credulity.

A second objection would hold that the metaphysics upon which Thomas's claim rests is itself the product of theological convictions, whether Christian or not. This objection is not un-like Derrida's use of the Heideggerian term 'onto-theology'. The full answer to the objection would be to retrace the route of metaphysics as it groped for a characterization of the divine. But the partial answer is that not every conviction is religious, and not every religious tenet is merely emotive. Hierarchy appears as a philosophical notion before it becomes religious. If *we* have difficulty thinking it clearly in philosophy, that is no mark against Aquinas.

The third possible objection would be more serious. It would argue that the problem of divine simplicity is in fact a pseudo-problem since it presupposes that language intends to be taken literally. If we use language all the time without importing on-tological distinctions, why should we worry about applying such language to God? There are two replies in Thomas to this objection. The first is that the objection merely restates Thomas's solution for the divine names — that is, the difference between the mode of meaning and the thing meant. But a second answer is more important. The objector fails to realize what is meant by "simplicity" when applied to God. This is a simplicity than which there could be no greater — a simplicity which abolishes the distinction which is fundamental to every creature, the distinction between *esse* and *essentia*. Knowing this, to go on applying complex sentences to God without raising the question of their appropriateness would be to abandon the wish for the veracity of language altogether.

The fourth and final objection would hold that it is impossible to stand within human thought and without it, to be at once bound to think in complexes and able to move beyond them to conceive of noncomplexes. How can Thomas meaningfully talk of what is absolutely simple if he is in principle unable to experience it in this life? The answer to that objection is the connection between the divine names and the problem of names *simpliciter*.

IV. Names and Divine Names

To the question how Thomas can end at a point which seems to stand outside language, one answer is that he begins at a point which is nearer the center of language. The doctrine of the divine names is earned by faithful attention to the varieties of human language in other cases — in the cases of metaphysics, mathematics, and physics, certainly, but even in the cases of buying five red apples or of teaching writing to the Nambikwara.[37] Aquinas can offer what seems an extravagant answer to the question of the divine names because he has a surer starting-point for the questions about names. It is surer in its rejection of a literalism of intelligibility, surer in its methodological restraint, and surer in its appreciation for lived variety. The Thomist doctrine of the divine names carries within it a view of the intelligibility of human language as secured by hierarchies of discourse, which, however much they are generated from below, are also secured by being limited at the top. The divine names are signs in language of that extralinguistic intelligibility which makes possible the varieties of linguistic signification. They cannot make that intelligibility present, but they can mark by varying absence the power of its effects.

The doctrine of the divine names stands, then, in the middle of a number of seemingly opposed Thomist doctrines. On the one hand, it is commonly Thomas's teaching that God cannot be known essentially by any human intellect in this life, that all speculative science about God is under the condition of the negative judgment, and that all human naming of God is radically flawed. On the other hand, he as frequently urges that God's knowledge of his own imitability is the ground of the intelligibility of creatures, that no speculative knowing stands except upon the foundation of metaphysics, and that the truth of human words or thoughts is only possible because of the prior truth of things in relation to God. The seeming contradiction of these doctrines is overcome by recognizing that the notion of hierarchy as such is constituted in the operation of both presence and absence.[38] Every act of approach is marked by a more sharply felt absence. The more intelligible the signified, the more inadequate the mode of signification. The greater the intelligibility of the mind's abstractive intention, the greater its distance from the existing things it seeks to understand. In these and many other instances hierarchies are constructed upon the opposition of the present image and the absent original. But the opposition persists only *because* the image is tied to the original. There would be no hierarchy if there were not both likeness and unlikeness.[39]

It is not only in the names of God that one sees shifts in the mode of signification. Such shifts occur at every level in the hierarchy of *scientiae*, in the reading of texts, and in ordinary speaking about the world. But there is more than this. It would not be un-Thomistic to say that the hierarchies in language are also constituted by being marked off one against the other. This is true in two different ways. Any predication, first, is a marking off, is a series of negations strung along behind the affirmation. As Thomas says against Maimonides: "In the name of any and every species is included the signification of a difference, by which there is excluded any other species which is divided from it" (*De pot.*, q. 7, a. 5, c, 198:2). But such differentiations are usually noted within a single level of the hierarchy. More interesting, second, are the larger differences by which the use of a mode of signification is made to distinguish one level from the others.

The distinction is made near the top of the hierarchy if one separates, e.g., the way in which a philosopher and a theologian consider creatures, even when speaking about the same "object." "If the (truths) concerning creatures are considered in common by the philosopher and the believer, they are presented on the basis of different starting-points" (2 *SCG*, c. 4, n. 4, 93:2). A similar modal difference is marked between the discourse of "metaphysics" as first philosophy and "metaphysics" as theology.[40] Below these highest discourses there are large differences in the expectations which can be brought to the understanding of any discourse. In a famous passage Aristotle remarks on the different expectations appropriate to different discourses: "In the same manner, then, ought one to accept each of the things said; for it belongs to the educated man (*pepaidemenou*) to seek for precision in each kind only so far as the nature of the thing allows; for it appears to be equally foolish to accept speaking calculated to persuade (*pithanalogountos*) from a mathematician and to demand demonstrations (*apodeixeis*) from a rhetorician" (*Nicomachean Ethics*, 1.3, 1094b2-7). Thomas comments: "Error would seem to be near at hand, (both) if someone were to accept a mathematician's using rhetorical persuasions, and if he were to expect sure demonstrations from a rhetorician, (demonstrations) such as the mathematician ought to offer. Both (errors) arise from this, that (the topic) is not considered in a manner appropriate to its matter" (*In eth.*, lib. 1, lect. 3, §36, 10:1-2). Thomas elsewhere adopts the Ciceronian distinction among the modes of rhetoric with their effects.[41] These are ordinary examples of the hierarchical disposition of speech.

There are other levels of discourse which figure decisively in the ascent to the divine. Chief among these is prayer. The simplest of the Christian prayers proclaims again in the middle of "ordinary" language that all discourses fall short of the highest things. Thomas writes that the Lord's prayer is the best prayer because it is "*secura,*" "*recta,*" "*ordinata,*" "*devota,*" and "*humilis.*"[42] When in the Lord's prayer one prays "hallowed be thy name," Thomas sees that one says four things. One says that the name of God is "*mirabile, amabile, venerabile, et inexplicabile*"; it is *inexplicabile* "since every tongue falls short of its telling."[43]

The hierarchy of human language culminates in the divine names. Their special place is due not only to the eminence of their object but also to their actualizing the final possibility of language itself. Long before Heidegger began using terms "under erasure," before Derrida borrowed the practice, the divine names were names which were always used "under erasure."[44] They were names which crossed themselves out. They were, in short, names which silenced themselves. This appearance of a sign of silence is not something mystical, or religious, or nonsensical. It is, in fact, the fulfillment of the possibility of the sign. This is where Derrida's charge against the traditional doctrine of the sign seems to fail badly.[45] The highest signs, the most important signs, have long been considered the most opaque. So it is with the divine names. Such signs must attempt to overcome their opacity in cancelling presence. But far from denying signification, they fulfill it. They prevent the idolatry of the sign, prevent the seduction by an illusory translucency of the sign. The failure of the divine names to make the signified present is their success as a pedagogical device. It becomes in Thomas, in fact, precisely the pedagogical device that Socratic irony is — and bears the same relation to the doctrine of sign in general.

If this suggestion is correct, then the existence of the divine names can be arrived at from within the hierarchy of other names. They are the necessary completion of the differentiated discourses about what is. They complete by admitting that the sign can never give directly the intelligible which lies beyond. In this way the names stand to the rest of human speaking as the metaphysical negative judgment stands to the rest of human knowing. Both are completing limitations. Both fulfill by making the transit to the intended object an act to be accomplished, not an act already done.

Let me say this again. Unless the signifier could finally cancel itself as a means of presence, the hierarchy of discourses would be impossible. The hierarchy is made possible by the play of the presence and absence of the signified through the signifier. The cancelling of the signifier in silence is the affirmation that there is a distance to be covered, a difference to be overcome. Without the transcendence of that signified "named" by the divine names, there would be neither distance nor difference, and so no possibility of hierarchy. The fact of a *hierarchy* of discourses constituted by a plurality of modes of signification requires the final absence of the signified in the sign.

This discovery in language is made sure by reflection on divine simplicity. Aquinas's monotheism is not so much the rejection of competing carved idols as it is the refusal to admit conceptual ones. The doctrine of the divine names falls out as the immediate consequence of this most important thing to be known about the divine nature. For this reason I think that the doctrine of the names is the surest philosophical approach to the nature of God. Any other treatment, unless it is placed after and under the doctrine of the names, is bound to fall into dialectical idolatry as a result of mistaking the logic of the terms which name divine attributes.

There may be, then, not only a metaphysics of *Exodus* but also a semantics of *Exodus*.[46] The entry of the name of God into speech discloses the hierarchy of language by signifying its absent ground. The establishment of the name of God, of the tablets of the Law, of the body of revealed texts, makes clear the refraction of language which had been present all along. "*Ego sum qui sum*" — the nature of God spoken, refracted, signified in absence, the name of God disclosing the being of every other name. This disclosure is the only sure access to God's nature. The absence of the signified behind the divine names is the clearest trace of God for embodied human knowing. The failure of the divine names is, then, both a grammar and a first philosophy.

NOTES

1. A complete account would require not only a much more detailed reading of antecedent and parallel texts but would also presuppose a surer grasp on Thomas's doctrine of philosophical discourses as semantic modes within the hierarchies of human language.

2. On this point I agree with certain contemporary critiques of the modern theory of sign — the obvious example would be Derrida, for whom see note 45 below. My agreement extends only to the critique of some modern views, since I take the major ancient and medieval accounts, at least before the fourteenth century, to be decisively different.

3. The loss of the names in considerations of analogy can be seen not only in Neo-Thomist works after Cajetan but also in analytic works which attempt to make the traditional account "rigorous." An example of the latter would be James F. Ross, "Analogy as a Rule of Meaning for Religious Language," *International Philosophical Quarterly* 1 (1961): 468-502. After the construction of quasi-rules for the Cajetanian types of analogy, Ross takes up the application of analogy to "religious language" only at the end, as a kind of lemma to the general theorem. This procedure seems to me not only to distort the balance of the parts of the doctrine but also to mistake its scope in restricting its effects to the "religious." The names are chiefly metaphysical and theological. As a corrective, see Ralph M. McInerny, *The Logic of Analogy: An Interpretation of St. Thomas* (The Hague: M. Nijhoff, 1961), pp. 153-65 and throughout.

4. According to the received chronology the questions *De potentia* were disputed in Rome in 1265-66. Work on the *Prima pars* of the *Summa theologiae* did not begin until 1266; the evidence of a citation in *ST*, 1, q. 79, a. 4, puts the composition of that portion after November 22, 1267. For the dates and the evidence in summary see James A. Weisheipl, *Friar Thomas d'Aquino* (Garden City, New York: Doubleday, 1974), pp. 361, 363.

5. For the doctrine in the *Sentences* see Eluthère Winance, "L'essence divine de la connaissance humaine dans le Commentaire sur les Sentences de Saint Thomas," *Revue Philosophique de Louvain* 55 (1957): 171-215. An account of apophasis based on the *Sentences* commentary can be had in Joseph Owens, "Aquinas — 'Darkness of Ignorance' in the Most Refined Notion of God," *Southwestern Journal of Philosophy* 5 (1974): 93-110. For the doctrine in the *Summa contra*

gentiles see Anton C. Pegis, *"Penitus manet ignotum," Mediaeval Studies* 27 (1965): 212-26. An essayist's account based largely on the *Summa theologiae* can be had in Raymond Laflamme, "Deux approches onomastiques de la théologie," *Laval Théologique Philosophique* 27 (1971): 111-28, where Thomas's achievement is seen as the balancing of "analogy" and "symbolism." The treatment of the names among Aquinas's Latin predecessors of the twelfth century is surveyed by M. D. Chenu, *La théologie au douzième siècle* (Paris: J. Vrin, 1957), pp. 100-7, where the connections with a general theory of language are emphasized. Twelfth-century accounts of the restrictions upon the presence of the divine in images can be had in Robert Javelet, *Image et ressemblance au douzième siècle* (Paris: Letouzey & Ané, 1967), especially 1: 125-27 and 246-97, where the emphasis is upon hierarchical participation and its failures.

6. I will use the edition of the *De potentia* by Paulus M. Pession in *Quaestiones disputatae*, vol. 2 (Turin and Rome: Marietti, 1965). Following the traditional citations, I will give the paragraph number (when available) and then the page and column from the Marietti edition.

7. See McInerny, *Logic of Analogy*, pp. 54-60, 157-58.

8. The principle that an effect is made in the likeness of its cause or, inversely, that a cause makes an effect in its own image is so common in Aquinas's texts that it has become a scholastic saw. Texts in which it appears include the commentary on the *Physics* (e.g., lib. 2, lect. 11, n. 2; lib. 2, lect. 10, n. 15), the commentary on *De anima* (lib. 3, lect. 14, n. 17; lib. 2, lect. 7, n. 9; lib. 3, lect. 6, n. 4), the *Sentences* lectures (*Sent.*, 1, d. 2, q. 1, a. 1; *Sent.*, 2, d. 14, q. 1, a. 2, ad 3m; *Sent.*, 3, d. 33, q. 1, a. 2, c) the *Summa contra gentiles* (*SCG*, 1, c. 37, n. 5; *SCG*, 2, c. 88, n. 5; *SCG*, 3, c. 52, n. 3; *SCG*, 4, c. 24, n. 8), and the great *Summa* (e.g., *ST*, 1, q. 33, a. 2, ad 4m; q. 35, a. 1, c). This principle is the center of the Thomist account of causation, and any attempt to replace it with a principle of "sufficient reason" must be regarded as a modern misunderstanding.

9. In stressing that the relation of causality is only a dependence in the effect, and in wishing to sanitize the Thomist doctrine on cosmological points, Lonergan makes difficulties for himself with causal likeness. See, e.g., *Grace and Freedom* (New York: Herder and Herder, 1971), ch. 4, where any consideration of likeness is muted.

10. On the importance of the principle for the doctrine of the names see Battista Mondin, "Il principio '*omne agens agit simile sibi*' e l'analogia dei nomi divini nel pensiero di S. Tommaso D'Aquino," *Divus Thomas* (Piacenza) 63 (1960): 336-48; and Thomas A. Fay, "The Problem of God-Language in Thomas Aquinas: What Can and Cannot Be Said," *Rivista di Filosofia Neo-Scholastica* 69 (1977): 385-89.

11. This is Thomas's usual teaching, except in *ST*, 1, q. 13, a. 11, ad 1m, where he holds that the name '*Tetragrammaton*' is superior to the name '*Qui est*' since it better signifies the incommunicability of the divine essence. On the sources of this doctrine in Maimonides see Armand Maurer, "St. Thomas on the Sacred Name 'Tetragrammaton'," *Mediaeval Studies* 34 (1972): 275-86.

12. Pession gives the reference to John Damascene as *De Fide Orthodoxa*, 1.12 (Marietti, 199:1). The reference ought rather to be to 1.9, where John speaks — following Gregory of Nyssa — of the whole of being as "*hoion ti pelagos ousias apeiron kai aoriston*" (1.9, lines 12-13, in the edition of Bonifatius Kotter, *Die Schriften des Johannes von Damaskos*, vol. 2 [Berlin and New York: Walter de Gruyter, 1973], p. 31). The phrase comes into Latin as "*velut pelagus substantiae infinitum*"; see the version of Burgundio in *De Fide Orthodoxa*, ed. Eligius M. Buytaert (St. Bonaventure, New York: Franciscan Institute; Louvain: E. Nauwelaerts; and Paderborn: F. Schöningh, 1955), 1.9, lines 16-17, page 49. For the sense of the phrase see Leo Sweeney, "John Damascene's 'Infinite Sea of Essence'," in *Studia Patristica*, vol. 6, ed. F. L. Cross, Texte und Untersuchungen zur Geschichte der altchristlichen Literatur, vol. 81 (Berlin: Akademie-Verlag, 1962), pp. 248-63. For the Patristic sources generally see C. J. De Vogel, " 'Ego sum qui sum' et sa signification pour une philosophie chrétienne," *Revue des Sciences Religieuses* 35 (1961): 346-53.

13. An argument that the divine names which refer to pure perfections *can* be treated as synonyms has been made by Johannes Bauer, "Können die Namen Gottes Synonyme sein? Mit besonderer Bezugnahme auf Thomas v. Aquin," *Salzburger Jahrbuch für Philosophie* 19 (1974): *Gedenkband zu Ehren des heiligen Thomas von Aquin (1274, 1974)*, ed. Zeno Bucher et al., pp. 83-91. But Bauer seems to miss the import of Thomas's doctrine that it is possible to know negatively the unity in God of such attributes without being able to think it positively.

14. See *SCG*, 1, cc. 30-33, then c. 34; *ST*, 1, q. 13, aa. 1-4, then a. 5.

15. Plotinus, *Enneads*, V.3.14.6-7, III.9.7.1-2, V.5.10-14, VI.9.3.41-49, VI.8.21.5-8, VI.9.10.19-11.4, and especially the ways of negation, analogy, and eminence in VI.7.36. Compare the tradition of commentary on Plato, *Parmenides*, 137C-142A. See R. T. Wallis, *Neoplatonism* (London: Duckworth, 1972), pp. 57-60, 88-89, 114-15, 118, 150-51, 158, 161, for a discussion of these passages and the development of the doctrine in the Porphyrian fragments, Iamblichus, and the Christian writers. With regard to the commentaries on the *Parmenides*, see Eugenio Corsini, *Il trattato De Divinis Nominibus dello Pseudo-Dionigi e i commenti neoplatonici al*

Parmenide (Turin: G. Giappichelli, 1962), especially pp. 115-22; and Stephen Gersh, *From Iamblichus to Eriugena* (Leiden: E. J. Brill, 1978), especially pp. 153-56.

16. The most detailed study of the Jewish and Islamic traditions with regard to the attributes comes in the many essays by Harry Austryn Wolfson, now anthologized by Isidore Twersky and George H. Williams as *Studies in the History of Philosophy and Religion*, vols. 1 and 2 (Cambridge, Massachusetts: Harvard University Press, 1973 and 1977). For Maimonides see especially *Studies*, 2: 195-230, 231-46, and 433-57; for the Islamic tradition, *Studies*, 1:143-69.

17. I will use the edition of the exposition *In librum Beati Dionysii De Divinis Nominibus* by Ceslaus Pera (Turin and Rome: Marietti, 1950), following the same practice of parenthetical reference (see note 5, above). The term '*artificialiter*' means here something positive, a work done well according to the skill of the best *artifex*. The use of the word, with its echoes from craftsmanship and artistry, may suggest something of how Thomas regards his own heuristic schemata.

18. Aquinas misunderstands the word '*hypotyposes*', glossing it as both "*characteres*" and "*distinctiones*" (*Div. Nom.*, Prooemium, 1, and c. 1, lect. 1, n. 3, 6:1). The word actually means something more like outlines or patterns.

19. Aquinas's refusal to move his exegesis away from the text of Dionysius is to be explained in part by the genre of the exposition and in part by the difficulties which he finds in the text (cf. prooemium, Marietti, 1-2). The extent to which Aquinas's doctrine is identical with that of Pseudo-Dionysius apart from the exposition is difficult to determine. See, on this question, Walter M. Neidel, *Thearchia: Die Frage nach dem Sinn von Gott bei Pseudo-Dionysius Areopagita und Thomas von Aquin* (Regensburg: Josef Habbel, 1976), pp. 1-29, where some of the difficulties are sketched; and Giovanni Bartolaso, "Originalità della teologia negativa secondo Tommaso d'Aquino," *Dio e l'economia della salvezza: Atti del congresso internazionale*, vol. 3 (Naples: Edizioni Domenicane Italiani, 1976), pp. 113-16. See also the earlier study of A. Feder, "Des Aquinaten Kommentar zu Pseudo-Dionysius 'De divinis Nominibus'," *Scholastik* 1 (1926): 321-51; and Werner Beierwaltes, "Der Kommentar zum *Liber de Causis* als neuplatonisches Element in der Philosophie des Thomas von Aquin," *Philosophisches Rundschau* 2 (1964): 192-215, where the question of the reworking is taken up in a larger context.

20. Jean-Luc Manion, *L'idole et la distance: Cinq études* (Paris: Bernard Grasset, 1977), p. 184.

21. Ibid., pp. 231, 184, and throughout.

22. Ibid., pp. 191-92, 195.

23. Ibid., pp. 186, 187, 199.

24. Ibid., pp. 232-41.

25. Manion's reading ought to be qualified by the more textually minded studies of René Roques, *L'univers dionysien: Structure hiérarchique du monde selon le Pseudo-Dénys* (Paris: Aubier, 1954); Eugenio Corsini, *Il trattato De Divinis Nominibus* (full citation in note 15, above); Ronald F. Hathaway, *Hierarchy and the Definition of Order in the Letters of Pseudo-Dionysius* (The Hague: M. Nijhoff, 1969); and Stephen Gersh, *From Iamblichus to Eriugena* (full citation in note 15, above), especially pp. 266-82.

26. On the history of the terms '*ablatio*' and '*remotio*' through Aquinas see the essay by Wolfson, "St. Thomas on Divine Attributes," in *Studies*, 2: 497-524, especially pp. 497-500. For one account of the steps in Aquinas's fundamental remotion see Owens, "Darkness of Ignorance," pp. 97-109.

27. See Leo Strauss, "How to Begin to Study the *Guide of the Perplexed*," in the translation of the *Guide* by Shlomo Pines (Chicago: University of Chicago Press, 1963), pp. xi-lvi; and the essay on Maimonides in Strauss, *Persecution and the Art of Writing* (Glencoe, Illinois: Free Press, 1952).

28. For example, *ST*, 1, q. 13, a. 2, c. But compare *De ver.*, q. 2, a. 3, c, where the reference is to the *Guide*, 3.19, and *SCG*, 2, c. 92, n. 12, where the reference is to the *Guide*, 2.6. Aquinas's knowledge of Maimonides is by no means restricted to the passages on the divine names.

29. Maimonides, *Guide*, 1.58; Pines tr., 1, p. 135.

30. Maimonides, *Guide*, 1.58; Pines tr., 1, p. 136.

31. A careful reading of the dedicatory epistle shows, I think, not only the ambiguities of Maimonides's relation to physics or metaphysics but also his assumption that the reader has been raised and formed in the community of the Torah; see Pines tr., 1, pp. 3-4. Recall also this remark from the introduction to the first book: "Or rather its purpose is to give indications to a religious man for whom the validity of our Law has become established in his soul and has become actual in his belief — such a man being perfect in his religion and character, and having studied the sciences of the philosophers and come to know what they signify" (Pines tr., 1, p. 5).

32. Bernhard Welte accuses Thomas of not following through on the project of a negative theology, despite his having announced it. Welte would find the working out of the project in Eckhart. See his "Bemerkungen zum Gottesbegriff des Thomas von Aquin," *Theologie und Glaube* 58 (1968): 409-16. I hope to defend Thomas's qualification of negation by hierarchy in the fourth section below.

33. For parallel passages on the doctrine of simplicity see *Sent.*, 1, d. 8, q. 4, a. 1; *SCG*, 1, c. 16 and c. 18; and *ST*, 1, q. 3, a. 7; on the doctrine of asymmetrical relations, *Sent.*, 1, d. 14, q. 1, a. 1; *SCG*, 2, c. 11; *ST*, 1, q. 13, a. 7, and q. 28, a. 1, and q. 34, a. 3.

34. Compare David Burrell, *Aquinas: God and Action* (Notre Dame, Indiana: University of Notre Dame Press, 1979), pp. 14-17, where the same point is made too emphatically, thus pushing the Thomist account over into that of Maimonides. A sounder contemporary treatment would be that of Karl Rahner, "Über die Unbegreiflichkeit Gottes bei Thomas von Aquin," in Ludger Oeing Hanhoff, ed., *Thomas von Aquin, 1274-1974* (Munich: Kosel, 1974), pp. 33-45. For a generally Thomistic treatment influenced by Maritain see J. H. Nicolas, *Dieu connu comme inconnu: essai d'une critique de la connaissance théologique* (Paris: Desclée de Brouwer, 1966).

35. E.g., Wallis, *Neoplatonism*, pp. 41-42.

36. *SCG*, 1, cc. 14-27, then c. 28; *ST*, 1, q. 3, aa. 1-8, then q. 4.

37. The last two instances are, of course, from Wittgenstein's *Investigations* and from Lévi-Strauss, *Tristes tropiques*, VII, 25, through Derrida, *De la grammatologie*, II, 1, pp. 149-202.

38. Presence and absence are made into one of the constitutive "couples" which ground philosophic thinking in Robert Sokolowski, *Presence and Absence* (Bloomington and London: Indiana University Press, 1978). Sokolowski touches on the names and on Aquinas in his final chapter, pp. 172-81. My own account differs from that of Sokolowski in the analysis of hierarchy and in the question of whether it is possible to "think beyond" the absence of the names.

39. My emphasis on the plurality of significations and on their ordering in hierarchical layers may remind some of Paul Ricoeur's definition of the symbol. See especially the essay "Existence and Hermeneutics," trans. Kathleen McLaughlin, in *The Conflict of Interpretations*, ed. Don Ihde (Evanston: Northwestern University Press, 1974), pp. 3-24. But Ricoeur's subordination (p. 12) of the "indirect, secondary, and figurative" meaning to the "direct, primary, literal meaning" reverses what I take to be the hierarchical order in Aquinas. For Aquinas all hierarchies, including the hierarchy of names, are grounded in the topmost member. Even if this is signified *quoad nos* in a derivative fashion, the correct understanding of the sign requires that one make the gesture of the inversion, of the correction which restores the "symbolically" signified to its primacy *quoad se*.

40. See, e.g., *In Boe. De Trin.*, q. 5, a. 4, and especially the ad 3m.

41. E.g., *ST*, 2-2, q. 177, a. 1, obj. 1; *In eth.*, lib. 1, lect. 18, n. 10.

42. *In Orationem Dominicam videlicet "Pater Noster" expositio*, prologus, in *Opuscula Theologica*, vol. 2 (Turin and Rome: Marietti, 1954), pp. 221-22, §§1019-25.

43. *In Orationem Dominicam*, Marietti, pp. 224-25, §§1044-47.

44. Martin Heidegger, *The Question of Being*, trans. W. Kluback and J. T. Wilde (New York: Harper & Row, 1958); Jacques Derrida, *De la grammatologie* (Paris: Les Editions de Minuit, 1967), pp. 31, 65, and so on. See Gayatri Spivak's introduction to the English transla-

tion, *Of Grammatology* (Baltimore and London: Johns Hopkins University Press, 1976), pp. xiv-xviii.

45. I have in mind specifically the passage in *De la grammatologie*, pp. 24-25; compare Spivak's version, p. 13. For a structurally similar reply to Derrida on literary grounds, and a rehabilitation of Rousseau, see Paul De Man, "Criticism and Crisis," in his *Blindness and Insight: Essays in the Rhetoric of Contemporary Criticism* (London: Oxford University Press, 1971).

46. There is, interestingly enough, a brief note by Gilson in which he stresses the importance of Maimonides's discussion of the attributes in the *Guide* (especially 1.58) as a source for Thomas's distinction between *esse* and *essentia*; see "Maimonide et la philosophie de l'*Exode*," *Mediaeval Studies* 13 (1951): 223-25.